The Life Experience
and
Gospel Labors

of the

RT. REV. RICHARD ALLEN

THE RT. REV. RICHARD ALLEN

The original of this portrait of Richard Allen hangs in historic St. George's Methodist Church, Fourth and Vine Streets, Philadelphia, Pennsylvania. Permission was granted to make a copy of the portrait.

THE LIFE EXPERIENCE
and
GOSPEL LABORS
of the
RT. REV. RICHARD ALLEN

To Which Is Annexed
The Rise and Progress of the African Methodist
Episcopal Church in the United States
of America

Containing a Narrative of the Yellow Fever
in the Year of Our Lord 1793

With an Address to the
PEOPLE OF COLOR IN THE UNITED STATES

Written by Himself
And Published by His Request

Mark the perfect man, and behold the upright: for
the end of that man is peace.—Ps. xxxvii, 37

With an Introduction by
GEORGE A. SINGLETON

Abingdon Press
Nashville

THE LIFE EXPERIENCE AND GOSPEL LABORS OF
THE RT. REV. RICHARD ALLEN

Library of Congress Cataloging in Publication Data
ALLEN, RICHARD, BP., 1760–1831.
  The life experience and gospel labors of the Rt. Rev. Richard
Allen.
  Reprint. Originally published: New York: Abingdon Press, 1960.
  1. Allen, Richard, Bp., 1760–1831. 2. African Methodist Episcopal
Church—Bishops—Biography. 3. Bishops—United States—Biogra-
phy. 4. African Methodist Episcopal Church—History. I. Title.
BX8459.A4A34   1983   287'.83 [B]   83-3728

ISBN 0-687-21844-6

MANUFACTURED BY THE PARTHENON PRESS AT
NASHVILLE, TENNESSEE, UNITED STATES OF AMERICA

Introduction

THIS BOOK contains the republished life story of Richard Allen, the illustrious founder of The African Methodist Episcopal Church. It is being sent forth in honor of the bicentennial of his birth. He was born February 14, 1760, at Philadelphia, a slave to a Quaker lawyer, the Honorable Benjamin Chew, Chief Justice of The Commonwealth of Pennsylvania, 1774-77. Allen was ten years old when the Boston Massacre occurred the night of March 5, 1770. Crispus Attucks, a runaway slave from Framingham, Massachussetts, was killed in the massacre, the first man to give his life for American independence.

The "doctrine of the rights of man" was in the atmosphere, and freely discussed. The American colonists were on the verge of fighting for freedom. Richard Allen was a product to this environment. When George Washington arrived in Philadelphia, he was met at the Gray's Ferry Crossing by a troop of cavalry which escorted him to the residence of Benjamin Chew at 110 South Third Street. Gathered beneath the hospitable roof were several of the most outstanding and famous personalities of the times— Benjamin Franklin, John Adams, Benjamin Rush, signers of the Declaration of Independence and framers of the Constitution. The youthful eyes and ears of Allen must have seen and heard much which enlightened and inspired him.

In the course of time, for financial reasons, Mr. Chew sold the Allen family to a Mr. Stokeley, near Dover, Delaware. In the year 1777, at the age of seventeen, Richard Allen was converted by the preaching of Freeborn Garrettson and joined the Methodist Society. He attended class meetings led by John Gray in the forest at Benjamin Wells's. Allen had a call to preach and was licensed in 1782. In 1783 he commenced traveling and proclaimed the gospel several years throughout the Middle Atlantic states. In 1799 he was ordained a deacon, and later an elder, by Francis Asbury. When the historic Christmas Conference met at Baltimore in 1784 to carry out John Wesley's plan to organize Methodism in the colonies, two Negro preachers were present: Richard Allen and "Black Harry," whose real name was Harry Hoosier. He had traveled with Thomas Coke and Asbury, and the former regarded him "as one of the best preachers in the world." Francis Asbury was elected a bishop, and John Dickins gave the Methodist Episcopal Church its name.

Richard Allen returned to the city of Philadelphia as a member of the Old St. George's Methodist Society at 4th and Vine Streets. He was given preaching assignments sometimes as early as five o'clock in the mornings. He preached often whenever and wherever he could, indoors and out-of-doors. He walked and rode horseback several miles to such towns as Atglen, Attleborough, Columbia, Ben-Salem, and Radnor, and delivered the Word of God to large and small audiences of whites, blacks, and integrated worshipers. At St. George he was a member of Class Number One, which met every Monday night. The leader was Blades Wildgoose.

The membership of the church increased. Many people of African descent attended the services. Once they outnumbered the whites. Gradually their presence became obnoxious, so they were placed around the walls on the main floor. Allen considered the attitude of increasing hostility, and in 1786 organized a group of forty-two among the oppressed within the church. One Sunday morning in the month of November, 1787, the year when the Constitution of the United States was drafted, Richard Allen and his friends went to St. George's to worship. They were met at the door by the sexton who directed them to the gallery, which in 1786 they had helped build with their contributions. They thought they would occupy relative places to the ones they had previously occupied on the main floor. The service began with singing, followed with prayer. While Allen and his friends were reverently kneeling, one of the officers attempted to pull Absalom Jones from his knees and told them they could not worship there. Allen raised his head and looked around. The group was threatened with expulsion; but when the prayer was over, Richard Allen walked out, followed by Absalom Jones, William White, and Dorus Ginnings. This was the beginning of The African Methodist Episcopal Church. Allen was not bitter or resentful, and remained a Methodist. He was a Christian.

The going out from St. George's Methodist Church was a supreme act of faith, for Allen like Abraham knew not where he was going. He trusted God, sought freedom of worship, personal dignity, and self-esteem. He was encouraged by such eminent white friends as Benjamin Rush and Robert Ralston. The first day they went out with a subscription list and raised $360. A storeroom was hired as a place of worship. Allen next purchased an old abandoned blacksmith shop for $35, and hauled it with his own team of six horses to a lot at the corner of Sixth and Lombard Streets which he himself bought from a Mark Wilcox. He dug the first spadeful of earth and repaired the shop for a house of God. When the church was built, it was dedicated by Francis Asbury, and John Dickins offered a prayer that it might be called "Bethel." Allen faced opposition from the officials of St. George who sought to control the movement, and from his own people, but he kept faith and moved steadily forward. He was not a weakling or a compromiser.

People of color in other areas faced similar problems to those which Richard Allen experienced. A few letters are extant which were exchanged between him and Daniel Coker of Baltimore. They are revealing of prejudice and segregation in the house of God. Therefore in April, 1816, Richard Allen called a meeting at Philadelphia for the purpose of taking some action. Fifteen preachers and laymen joined with him.

From Baltimore: The Rev. Daniel Coker, Richard Williams, and Henry Harden. Messrs. Edward Williamson, Stephen Hill, and Nichols Gillard.

From Philadelphia: The Rev. Richard Allen, Clayton Durham, Jacob Tapsico, James Champion, and Thomas Webster.

From Attleborough, Pennsylvania: The Rev. Jacob Marsh, William Anderson, and Edward Jackson.

From Wilmington, Delaware: The Rev. Peter Spencer.

From Salem, New Jersey: Reuben Cuff.

Richard Allen, the first ordained preacher of African descent in America, was elected bishop *in absentia.* Both he and Daniel Coker were elected the first day, but when Allen appeared the second day he

8

took the position that two bishops were not needed at the time of organization. Coker resigned, and Allen was set apart. The church which he organized nearly one and three-quarter centuries ago, and formed into a connection a hundred and forty-four years ago, has grown to over a million members and adherents in the United States of America (including the new state, Alaska), Canada, Bermuda, the West Indies, South America, and West and South Africa.

By his contribution Richard Allen has become the precious ideal of all religious groups and denominations which prize manhood, equality, and the intrinsic worth of human personality, regardless of race, color, or creed. He is the symbol of patriotism, for he was a noncombatant in the Revolutionary War and hauled salt for George Washington's army from Rehoboth, Delaware. During the War of 1812 he raised a Black Legion of troops to help defend the newly formed nation. In one of the conflicts his brother lost his life. The church which Richard Allen organized is a universal symbol, with the motto: "God Our Father, Christ Our Redeemer, Man Our Brother."

In honoring Richard Allen on the bicentennial of his birth we enshrine his memory on the heights. A tomb holds his sacred dust in the northwest corner of the basement of Mother Bethel, Philadelphia. He died March 26, 1831, but lives eternally. The words of B. W. Arnett, after having visited the tomb March 6, 1867, are ours:

Men will travel hundreds of miles, over freezing snow and scorching sand, to behold the place where a poet first breathed the air; they will journey to the tombs of mighty heroes. The Mohammedan thinks he must visit Mecca once during his lifetime, in order that he may receive the smiles of Allah! The ancient Jew went annually to the City of David. The patriotic American embraces every opportunity to visit the grave of Washington. The Freedman of the South raises his devotional window toward the tomb of Lincoln, and teaches his children to visit the sepulchre of the giant Emancipator. The Christian, though not permitted to visit the place where Jesus is, yet he may visit the tomb where he once lay. In the same spirit I invite the communicant and friend of Bethel to come with me, and let us visit the sacred tomb of Richard Allen, the first Bishop of the A. M. E. Church. Though no costly pile of granite attracts the passing throng, no ostentatious status of brass marks the place where sacred worth is enshrined; nor is there any finely written epitaph to speak of his fame, yet let us approach the sacred spot in reverential awe. There is the tomb! what glorious reminiscence! what sweet recollections of the departed great! There is the mother church standing in unaustentious splendor; and while I stand soliloquising about the past and the present, I look once more upon the temple, and wonder how many have gone from it to join the saints above. Imagination starts up and annihilates time and space, brings the holy hands before me in all the vividness of life; and while I look and contemplate, away ye profane! Ye souls, whose lives are folly and mirth, disturb me not in my reverie; and ye who have no taste for the spiritual, away! and let me meditate upon the saint of the living God! We ask the pure in heart, and specially the ministers of Christ, to come and stand at the sacred tomb, and see if they cannot learn a lesson of incalculable benefit.

Though the white slab of marble and few brick hide from mortal view all that remains of the Bishop, yet I feel to rejoice in the belief that his spirit has mounted above; and is now pleading for the preservation of the Church he organized—our beloved Bethel.

This feeble effort is dedicated to the Class of Bishops of 1908, elected at Norfolk, Virginia: Edward Wilkerson Lampton, Henry Blanton Parks, Joseph Simeon Flipper, William Henry Heard, and John Albert Johnson. At the Centennial General Conference of 1916 in Philadelphia they established a Scholarship for Graduate Study in Theology. I was humbly one of the recipients. I am grateful beyond words to "Monnaie," my beloved wife, for her contribution as a typist, her encouragement and co-operation.

GEORGE A. SINGLETON, Secretary
of The Commission on the 200th Anniversary
of the Birth of Richard Allen

Preface

A GREAT part of this work having been written many years after events actually took place, and as my memory could not point out the exact time of many occurrences, they are, however (as many as I can recollect), pointed out; some without day or date, which, I presume, will be of no material consequence so that they are confined to the truth.

Could I but recollect the half of my trials and sufferings in this life, with the many meetings I have held, and the various occurrences that have taken place in my travelling to and fro, preaching the Gospel of our Lord and Saviour Jesus Christ, to Adam's lost race, they would swell this little book far beyond my inclination, and weary perhaps those into whose hands it may chance to come; but as I have been earnestly solicited by many of my friends to leave a small detail of my life and proceedings, I have thought proper, for the satisfaction of those who (after I am dead and in the grave) may feel an inclination to learn the commencement of my life, to leave behind me this short account for their perusal.

Richard Allen

Life, Experience, Etc.,
of the
RT. REV. RICHARD ALLEN

I WAS born in the year of our Lord 1760, on February 14th, a slave to Benjamin Chew, of Philadelphia. My mother and father and four children of us were sold into Delaware state, near Dover; and I was a child and lived with him until I was upwards of twenty years of age, during which time I was awakened and brought to see myself, poor, wretched and undone, and without the mercy of God must be lost. Shortly after, I obtained mercy through the blood of Christ, and was constrained to exhort my old companions to seek the Lord. I went rejoicing for several days and was happy in the Lord, in conversing with many old, experienced Christians. I was brought under doubts, and was tempted to believe I was deceived, and was constrained to seek the Lord afresh. I went with my head bowed down for many days. My sins were a heavy burden. I was tempted to believe there was no mercy for me. I cried to the Lord both night and day. One night I thought hell would be my portion. I cried unto Him who delighteth to hear the prayers of a poor sinner, and all of a sudden my dungeon shook, my chains flew off, and, glory to God, I cried. My soul was filled. I cried, enough for me—the Saviour died. Now my confidence was strengthened that the Lord, for Christ's sake, had heard my prayers and pardoned all my sins. I was constrained to go from house to house, exhorting my old companions, and telling to all around what a dear Saviour I had found. I joined the Methodist Society and met in class at Benjamin Wells's, in the forest, Delaware state. John Gray was the class leader. I met in his class for several years.

My master was an unconverted man, and all the family, but he was what the world called a good master. He was more like a father to his slaves than anything else. He was a very tender, humane man. My mother and father lived with him for many years. He was brought into difficulty, not being able to pay for us, and mother having several children after he had bought us, he sold my mother and three children. My mother sought the Lord and found favor with him, and became a very pious woman. There were three children of us remained with our old master. My oldest brother embraced religion and my sister. Our neighbors, seeing that our master indulged us with the privilege of attending meeting once in two weeks, said that Stokeley's Negroes would soon ruin him; and so my brother and myself held a council together, that we would attend more faithfully to our master's business, so that it should not be said that religion made us worse servants; we would work night and day to get our crops forward, so that they should be disappointed. We frequently went to meeting on every other Thursday; but if we were likely to be backward with our crops we would refrain from going to meeting. When our master found we were making no provision to go to meeting, he would frequently ask us if it was not our meeting day, and if we were not going. We would frequently tell him: "No, sir, we would rather stay at home and get our

16

work done." He would tell us: "Boys, I would rather
you would go to your meeting; if I am not good myself, I like to see you striving yourselves to be good."
Our reply would be: "Thank you, sir, but we would
rather stay and get our crops forward." So we always continued to keep our crops more forward than
our neighbors, and we would attend public preaching once in two weeks, and class meeting once a week.
At length, our master said he was convinced that religion made slaves better and not worse, and often
boasted of his slaves for their honesty and industry.
Some time after, I asked him if I might ask the
preachers to come and preach at his house. He being
old and infirm, my master and mistress cheerfully
agreed for me to ask some of the Methodist preachers
to come and preach at his house. I asked him for a
note. He replied, if my word was not sufficient, he
should send no note. I accordingly asked the preacher.
He seemed somewhat backward at first, as my master
did not send a written request; but the class leader
(John Gray) observed that my word was sufficient; so
he preached at my old master's house on the next
Wednesday. Preaching continued for some months;
at length, Freeborn Garrettson preached from these
words, "Thou art weighed in the balance, and art
found wanting." In pointing out and weighing the
different characters, and among the rest weighed the
slaveholders, my master believed himself to be one
of that number, and after that he could not be satisfied to hold slaves, believing it to be wrong. And
after that he proposed to me and my brother buying
our times, to pay him 60£. gold and silver, or $2000,
Continental money, which we complied with in the
year 17——.

We left our master's house, and I may truly say it
was like leaving our father's house; for he was a kind,

affectionate and tender-hearted master, and told us to make his house our home when we were out of a place or sick. While living with him we had family prayer in the kitchen, to which he frequently would come out himself at time of prayer, and my mistress with him. At length he invited us from the kitchen to the parlor to hold family prayer, which we attended to. We had our stated times to hold our prayer meetings and give exhortations at in the neighborhood.

I had it often impressed upon my mind that I should one day enjoy my freedom; for slavery is a bitter pill, notwithstanding we had a good master. But when we would think that our day's work was never done, we often thought that after our master's death we were liable to be sold to the highest bidder, as he was much in debt; and thus my troubles were increased, and I was often brought to weep between the porch and the altar. But I have had reason to bless my dear Lord that a door was opened unexpectedly for me to buy my time and enjoy my liberty. When I left my master's house I knew not what to do, not being used to hard work, what business I should follow to pay my master and get my living. I went to cutting of cord wood. The first day my hands were so blistered and sore, that it was with difficulty I could open or shut them. I kneeled down upon my knees and prayed that the Lord would open some way for me to get my living. In a few days, my hands recovered and became accustomed to cutting of wood and other hardships; so I soon became able to cut my cord and a half and two cords a day. After I was done cutting I was employed in a brickyard by one Robert Register, at $50 a month, Continental money. After I was done with the brickyard I went to days' work, but did not forget to serve my dear Lord. I used ofttimes to pray, sitting, standing or lying; and while my hands were employed to earn my bread, my heart was devoted to my dear Redeemer. Sometimes I would awake from my sleep, preaching and praying. I was after this employed in driving of wagon in time of the Continental war, in drawing salt from Rehoboth, Sussex County, in Delaware. I had my regular stops and preaching places on the road. I enjoyed many happy seasons in meditation and prayer while in this employment.

After peace was proclaimed, I then travelled extensively, striving to preach the Gospel. My lot was cast in Wilmington. Shortly after, I was taken sick with the fall fever and then the pleurisy. September the 3rd 1783, I left my native place. After leaving Wilmington, I went into New Jersey, and there traveled and strove to preach the Gospel until the spring of 1784. I then became acquainted with Benjamin Abbott, that great and good apostle. He was one of the greatest men that ever I was acquainted with. He seldom preached but what there were souls added to his labor. He was a man of as great faith as any that ever I saw. The Lord was with him, and blessed his labors abundantly. He was a friend and father to me. I was sorry when I had to leave West Jersey, knowing I had to leave a father. I was employed in cutting of wood for Captain Cruenkleton, although I preached the Gospel at nights and on Sundays. My dear Lord was with me, and blessed my labors—Glory to God—and gave me souls for my hire. I then visited East Jersey, and labored for my dear Lord, and became acquainted with Joseph Budd, and made my home with him, near the mills—a family, I trust, who loved and served the Lord. I labored some time there, but being much afflicted in body with the inflammatory rheumatism, was not so successful as in some other places. I went from there to Jonathan

19

Bunn's near Bennington, East New Jersey. There I labored in that neighborhood for some time. I found him and his family kind and affectionate, and he and his dear wife were a father and mother of Israel. In the year 1784, I left East Jersey and labored in Pennsylvania. I walked until my feet became so sore and blistered the first day, that I scarcely could bear them to the ground. I found the people very humane and kind in Pennsylvania. I having but little money, I stopped at Caesar Waters's, at Radnor township, twelve miles from Philadelphia. I found him and his wife very kind and affectionate to me. In the evening they asked me if I would come and take tea with them; but after sitting awhile, my feet became so sore and painful that I could scarcely be able to put them to the floor. I told them that I would accept their kind invitation, but my feet pained me so that I could not come to the table. They brought the table to me. Never was I more kindly received by strangers that I had never before seen, than by them. She bathed my feet with warm water and bran; the next morning my feet were better and free from pain. They asked me if I would preach for them. I preached for them the next evening. We had a glorious meeting. They invited me to stay till Sabbath day, and preach for them. I agreed to do so, and preached on Sabbath day to a large congregation of different persuasions, and my dear Lord was with me, and I believe there were many souls cut to the heart, and were added to the ministry. They insisted on me to stay longer with them. I stayed and labored in Radnor several weeks. Many souls were awakened and cried aloud to the Lord to have mercy upon them. I was frequently called upon by many inquiring what they should do to be saved. I appointed them to prayer and supplication at the throne of grace, and to make use of all manner of prayer, and pointed them to the invitation of our Lord and Saviour, Jesus Christ, who has said: "Come unto me, all ye that are weary and heavy laden, and I will give you rest." Glory be to God! and now I know he was a God at hand and not afar off. I preached my farewell sermon, and left these dear people. It was a time of visitation from above, many were the slain of the Lord. Seldom did I ever experience such a time of mourning and lamentation among a people. There were but few colored people in the neighborhood—the most of my congregation was white. Some said, "this man must be a man of God, I never heard such preaching before." We spent a greater part of the night in singing and prayer with the mourners. I expected I should have had to walk, as I had done before; but Mr. Davis had a creature that he made a present to me; but I intended to pay him for his horse if ever I got able. My dear Lord was kind and gracious to me. Some years after I got into business and thought myself able to pay for the horse. The horse was too light and small for me to travel on far. I traded it away with George Huftman for a blind horse but larger. I found my friend Huftman very kind and affectionate to me, and his family also. I preached several times at Huftman's meeting-house to a large and numerous congregation.

I proceeded on to Lancaster, Pennsylvania. I found the people in general dead to religion and scarcely a form of godliness. I went on to Little York, and put up at George Tess's, a sadler, and I believed him to be a man that loved and served the Lord. I had comfortable meetings with the Germans. I left Little York and proceeded on to the state of Maryland, and stopped at Mr. Benjamin Grover's; and I believed him to be a man that loved and served the Lord. I

21

had many happy seasons with my dear friends. His wife was a very pious woman; but their dear children were strangers to vital religion. I preached in the neighborhood for some time, and travelled Hartford circuit with Mr. Porters, who travelled that circuit. I found him very useful to me. I also travelled with Jonathan Forest and Leari Coal.

December 1784, General Conference sat in Baltimore, the first General Conference ever held in America. The English preachers just arrived from Europe were, Rev. Dr. Coke, Richard Whatcoat and Thomas Vassey. This was the beginning of the Episcopal Church amongst the Methodists. Many of the ministers were set apart in holy orders at this conference, and were said to be entitled to the gown; and I have thought religion has been declining in the church ever since. There was a pamphlet published by some person, which stated, that when the Methodists were no people, then they were a people; and now they have become a people they were no people; which had often serious weight upon my mind.

In 1785 the Rev. Richard Whatcoat was appointed on Baltimore circuit. He was, I believe, a man of God. I found great strength in travelling with him— a father in Israel. In his advice he was fatherly and friendly. He was of a mild and serene disposition. My lot was cast in Baltimore, in a small meeting-house called Methodist Alley. I stopped at Richard Mould's, and was sent to my lodgings, and lodged at Mr. McCannon's. I had some happy meetings in Baltimore. I was introduced to Richard Russell, who was very kind and affectionate to me, and attended several meetings. Rev. Bishop Asbury sent for me to meet him at Henry Gaff's. I did so. He told me he wished me to travel with him. He told me that in the slave countries, Carolina and other places, I must not intermix with the slaves, and I would frequently have to sleep in his carriage, and he would allow me my victuals and clothes. I told him I would not travel with him on these conditions. He asked me my reason. I told him if I was taken sick, who was to support me? and that I thought people ought to lay up something while they were able, to support themselves in time of sickness or old age. He said that was as much as he got, his victuals and clothes. I told him he would be taken care of, let his afflictions be as they were, or let him be taken sick where he would, he would be taken care of; but I doubted whether it would be the case with myself. He smiled, and told me he would give me from then until he returned from the eastward to make up my mind, which would be about three months. But I made up my mind that I would not accept of his proposals. Shortly after I left Hartford Circuit, and came to Pennsylvania, on Lancaster circuit. I travelled several months on Lancaster circuit with the Rev. Peter Morratte and Irie Ellis. They were very kind and affectionate to me in building me up; for I had many trials to pass through, and I received nothing from the Methodist connection. My usual method was, when I would get bare of clothes, to stop travelling and go to work, so that no man could say I was chargeable to the connection. My hands administered to my necessities. The autumn of 1785 I returned again to Radnor. I stopped at George Giger's, a man of God, and went to work. His family were all kind and affectionate to me. I killed seven beeves, and supplied the neighbors with meat; got myself pretty well clad through my own industry —thank God—and preached occasionally. The elder in charge in Philadelphia frequently sent for me to come to the city. February, 1786, I came to Philadelphia. Preaching was given out for me at five o'clock

23

in the morning at St. George church. I strove to preach as well as I could, but it was a great cross to me; but the Lord was with me. We had a good time, and several souls were awakened, and were earnestly seeking redemption in the blood of Christ. I thought I would stop in Philadelphia a week or two. I preached at different places in the city. My labor was much blessed. I soon saw a large field open in seeking and instructing my African brethren, who had been a long forgotten people and few of them attended public worship. I preached in the commons, in Southwark, Northern Liberties, and wherever I could find an opening. I frequently preached twice a day, at 5 o'clock in the morning and in the evening, and it was not uncommon for me to preach from four to five times a day. I established prayer meetings; I raised a society in 1786 for forty-two members. I saw the necessity of erecting a place of worship for the colored people. I proposed it to the most respectable people of color in this city; but here I met with opposition. I had but three colored brethren that united with me in erecting a place of worship—the Rev. Absalom Jones, William White and Dorus Ginnings. These united with me as soon as it became public and known by the elder who was stationed in the city. The Rev. C———B——— opposed the plan, and would not submit to any argument we could raise; but he was shortly removed from the charge. The Rev. Mr. W——— took the charge, and the Rev. L——— G———. Mr. W——— was much opposed to an African church, and used very degrading and insulting language to us, to try and prevent us from going on. We all belonged to St. George's church—Rev. Absalom Jones, William White and Dorus Ginnings. We felt ourselves much cramped; but my dear Lord was with us, and we believed, if it was his will, the

24

work would go on, and that we would be able to succeed in building the house of the Lord. We established prayer meetings and meetings of exhortation, and the Lord blessed our endeavors, and many souls were awakened; but the elder soon forbid us holding any such meetings; but we viewed the forlorn state of our colored brethren, and that they were destitute of a place of worship. They were considered as a nuisance.

A number of us usually attended St. George's church in Fourth street; and when the colored people began to get numerous in attending the church, they moved us from the seats we usually sat on, and placed us around the wall, and on Sabbath morning we went to church and the sexton stood at the door, and told us to go in the gallery. He told us to go, and we would see where to sit. We expected to take the seats over the ones we formerly occupied below, not knowing any better. We took those seats. Meeting had begun, and they were nearly done singing, and just as we got to the seats, the elder said, "Let us pray." We had not been long upon our knees before I heard considerable scuffling and low talking. I raised my head up and saw one of the trustees, H———M———, having hold of the Rev. Absalom Jones, pulling him up off of his knees, and saying, "You must get up—you must not kneel here." Mr. Jones replied, "Wait until prayer is over." Mr. H——— M——— said "No, you must get up now, or I will call for aid and force you away." Mr. Jones said, "Wait until prayer is over, and I will get up and trouble you no more." With that he beckoned to one of the other trustees, Mr. L——— S——— to come to his assistance. He came, and went to William White to pull him up. By this time prayer was over, and we all went out of the church in a body, and they were no more plagued with us in the church. This raised a great excitement and in-

25

quiry among the citizens, in so much that I believe they were ashamed of their conduct. But my dear Lord was with us, and we were filled with fresh vigor to get a house erected to worship God in. Seeing our forlorn and distressed situation, many of the hearts of our citizens were moved to urge us forward; notwithstanding we had subscribed largely towards finishing St. George's church, in building the gallery and laying new floors, and just as the house was made comfortable, we were turned out from enjoying the comforts of worshipping therein. We then hired a store-room, and held worship by ourselves. Here we were pursued with threats of being disowned, and read publicly out of meeting if we did continue worship in the place we had hired; but we believed the Lord would be our friend. We got subscription papers out to raise money to build the house of the Lord. By this time we had waited on Dr. Rush and Mr. Robert Ralston, and told them of our distressing situation. We considered it a blessing that the Lord had put it into our hearts to wait upon those gentlemen. They pitied our situation, and subscribed largely towards the church, and were very friendly towards us, and advised us how to go on. We appointed Mr. Ralston our treasurer. Dr. Rush did much for us in public by his influence. I hope the name of Dr. Benjamin Rush and Robert Ralston will never be forgotten among us. They were the first two gentlemen who espoused the cause of the oppressed, and aided us in building the house of the Lord for the poor Africans to worship in. Here was the beginning and rise of the first African church in America. But the elder of the Methodist Church still pursued us. Mr. John McClaskey called upon us and told us if we did not erase our names from the subscription paper, and give up the paper, we would be publicly turned out of meeting. We asked

him if we had violated any rules of discipline by so
doing. He replied, "I have the charge given to me by
the Conference, and unless you submit I will read you
publicly out of meeting." We told him we were willing to abide by the discipline of the Methodist Church,
"And if you will show us where we have violated any
law of discipline of the Methodist Church, we will
submit; and if there is no rule violated in the discipline we will proceed on." He replied, "We will
read you all out." We told him if he turned us out
contrary to rule of discipline, we should seek further
redress. We told him we were dragged off of our
knees in St. George's church, and treated worse than
heathens; and we were determined to seek out for ourselves, the Lord being our helper. He told us we were
not Methodists, and left us. Finding we would go on in
raising money to build the church, he called upon us
again, and wished to see us all together. We met him.
He told us that he wished us well, that he was a
friend to us, and used many arguments to convince us
that we were wrong in building a church. We told him
we had no place of worship; and we did not mean to
go to St. George's church any more, as we were so
scandalously treated in the presence of all the congregation present; "and if you deny us your name, you
cannot seal up the scriptures from us, and deny us
a name in heaven. We believe heaven is free for all
who worship in spirit and truth." And he said, "So
you are determined to go on." We told him "Yes, God
being our helper." He then replied, "We will disown
you all from the Methodist connection." We believed
if we put our trust in the Lord, he would stand by us.
This was a trial that I never had to pass through before. I was confident that the great head of the church
would support us. My dear Lord was with us. We
went out with our subscription paper, and met with

27

great success. We had no reason to complain of the liberality of the citizens. The first day the Rev. Absalom Jones and myself went out we collected three hundred and sixty dollars. This was the greatest day's collection that we met with. We appointed a committee to look out for a lot—the Rev. Absalom Jones, William Gray, William Wilcher and myself. We pitched upon a lot at the corner of Lombard and Sixth streets. They authorized me to go and agree for it. I did accordingly. The lot belonged to Mr. Mark Wilcox. We entered into articles of agreement for the lot. Afterwards the committee found a lot in Fifth street, in a more commodious part of the city, which we bought; and the first lot they threw upon my hands, and wished me to give it up. I told them they had authorized me to agree for the lot, and they were all well satisfied with the agreement I had made, and I thought it was hard that they would throw it upon my hands. I told them I would sooner keep it myself than to forfeit the agreement I had made. And so I did.

We bore much persecution from many of the Methodist connection; but we have reason to be thankful to Almighty God, who was our deliverer. The day was appointed to go and dig the cellar. I arose early in the morning and addressed the throne of grace, praying that the Lord would bless our endeavors. Having by this time two or three teams of my own—as I was the first proposer of the African church, I put the first spade in the ground to dig a cellar for the same. This was the first African Church or meetinghouse that was erected in the United States of America. We intended it for the African preaching-house or church; but finding that the elder stationed in this city was such an opposer to our proceedings of erecting a place of worship, though the principal part of the directors of this church belonged to the Methodist connection, the elder stationed here would neither preach for us, nor have anything to do with us. We then held an election, to know what religious denomination we should unite with. At the election it was determined—there were two in favor of the Methodist, the Rev. Absalom Jones and myself, and a large majority in favor of the Church of England. The majority carried. Notwithstanding we had been so violently persecuted by the elder, we were in favor of being attached to the Methodist connection; for I was confident that there was no religious sect or denomination would suit the capacity of the colored people as well as the Methodist; for the plain and simple gospel suits best for any people; for the unlearned can understand, and the learned are sure to understand; and the reason that the Methodist is so successful in the awakening and conversion of the colored people, the plain doctrine and having a good discipline. But in many cases the preachers would act to please their own fancy, without discipline, till some of them became such tyrants, and more especially to the colored people. They would turn them out of society, giving them no trial, for the smallest offense, perhaps only hearsay. They would frequently, in meeting the class, impeach some of the members of whom they had heard an ill report, and turn them out, saying, "I have heard thus and thus of you, and you are no more a member of society"— without witnesses on either side. This has been frequently done, notwithstanding in the first rise and progress in Delaware state, and elsewhere, the colored people were their greatest support; for there were but few of us free; but the slaves would toil in their little patches many a night until midnight to raise their little truck and sell to get something to support them more than what their masters gave them, but

29

we used often to divide our little support among the white preachers of the Gospel. This was once a quarter. It was in the time of the old Revolutionary War between Great Britain and the United States. The Methodists were the first people that brought glad tidings to the colored people. I feel thankful that ever I heard a Methodist preach. We are beholden to the Methodists, under God, for the light of the Gospel we enjoy; for all other denominations preached so high-flown that we were not able to comprehend their doctrine. Sure am I that reading sermons will never prove so beneficial to the colored people as spiritual or extempore preaching. I am well convinced that the Methodist has proved beneficial to thousands and ten times thousands. It is to be awfully feared that the simplicity of the Gospel that was among them fifty years ago, and that they conform more to the world and the fashions thereof, they would fare very little better than the people of the world. The discipline is altered considerably from what it was. We would ask for the good old way, and desire to walk therein.

In 1793 a committee was appointed from the African Church to solicit me to be their minister, for there was no colored preacher in Philadelphia but myself. I told them I could not accept of their offer, as I was a Methodist. I was indebted to the Methodists, under God, for what little religion I had; being convinced that they were the people of God, I informed them that I could not be anything else but a Methodist, as I was born and awakened under them, and I could go no further with them, for I was a Methodist, and would leave you in peace and love. I would do nothing to retard them in building a church as it was an extensive building, neither would I go out with a subscription paper until they were done going out

with their subscription. I bought an old frame that
had been formerly occupied as a blacksmith shop,
from Mr. Sims, and hauled it on the lot in Sixth near
Lombard street, that had formely been taken for the
Church of England. I employed carpenters to repair
the old frame, and fit it for a place of worship. In
July 1794, Bishop Asbury being in town I solicited
him to open the church* for us which he accepted.
The Rev. John Dickins sung and prayed, and Bishop
Asbury preached. The house was called Bethel, agreeable to the prayer that was made. Mr. Dickins prayed
that it might be a bethel** to the gathering in of
thousands of souls. My dear Lord was with us, so
that there were many hearty "amen's" echoed through
the house. This house of worship has been favored
with the awakening of many souls, and I trust they
are in the Kingdom, both white and colored. Our war-
fare and troubles now began afresh. Mr. C. proposed
that we should make over the church to the Conference. This we objected to; he asserted that we could
not be Methodists unless we did; we told him he might
deny us their name, but they could not deny us a seat
in Heaven. Finding that he could not prevail with us
so to do, he observed that we had better be incorporated, then we could get any legacies that were left
for us, if not, we could not. We agreed to be incorporated. He offered to draw the incorporation himself,
that it would save us the trouble of paying for to get
it drawn. We cheerfully submitted to his proposed
plan. He drew the incorporation, but incorporated
our church under the Conference, our property was
then all consigned to the Conference for the present

* This church will at present accommodate between 3,000
and 4,000 persons.
** See Genesis Chapter 28.

31

bishops, elders, ministers, etc., that belonged to the white Conference, and our property was gone. Being ignorant of incorporations we cheerfully agreed thereto. We labored about ten years under this incorporation, until James Smith was appointed to take the charge in Philadelphia; he soon waked us up by demanding the keys and books of the church, and forbid us holding any meetings except by orders from him; these propositions we told him we could not agree to. He observed he was elder, appointed to the charge, and unless we submitted to him, he would read us all out of meeting. We told him the house was ours, we had bought it, and paid for it. He said he would let us know it was not ours, it belonged to the Conference; we took counsel on it; counsel informed us we had been taken in; according to the incorporation it belonged to the white connection. We asked him if it couldn't be altered; he told us if two-thirds of the society agreed to have it altered, it could be altered. He gave me a transcript to lay before them; I called the society together and laid it before them. My dear Lord was with us. It was unanimously agreed to, by both male and female. We had another incorporation drawn that took the church from Conference, and got it passed, before the elder knew anything about it. This raised a considerable rumpus, for the elder contended that it would not be good unless he had signed it. The elder, with the trustees of St. George's, called us together, and said we must pay six hundred dollars a year for their services, or they could not serve us. We told them we were not able so to do. The trustees of St. George's insisted that we should or should not be supplied by their preachers. At last they made a move that they would take four hundred; we told them that our house was considerably in debt, and we were poor people, and we could not agree to pay four hundred, but we agreed to give them two hundred. It was moved by one of the trustees of St. George's that the money should be paid into their treasury; we refused paying it into their treasury, but we would pay it to the preacher that served; they made a move that the preacher should not receive the money from us. The Bethel trustees made a move that their funds should be shut and they would pay none; this caused a considerable contention. At length they withdrew their motion. The elder supplied us preaching five times in a year for two hundred dollars. Finding that they supplied us so seldom, the trustees of Bethel church passed a resolution that they would pay but one hundred dollars a year, as the elder only preached five times in a year for us; they called for the money, we paid him twenty-five dollars a quarter, but he being dissatisfied, returned the money back again, and would not have it unless we paid him fifty dollars. The trustees concluded it was enough for five sermons, and said they would pay no more; the elder of St. George's was determined to preach for us no more, unless we gave him two hundred dollars, and we were left alone for upwards of one year.

Mr. Samuel Royal being appointed to the charge of Philadelphia, declared unless we should repeal the Supplement, neither he nor any white preacher, travelling or local, should preach any more for us; so we were left to ourselves. At length the preachers and stewards belonging to the Academy, proposed serving us on the same terms that we had offered to the St. George's preachers, and they preached for us better than twelve months, and then demanded $150 per year; this not being complied with, they declined preaching for us, and we were once more left to ourselves, as an edict was passed by the elder, that if any local preacher should serve us, he should be expelled

33

from the connection. John Emory, then elder of the Academy, published a circular letter, in which we were disowned by the Methodists. A house was also hired and fitted up for worship, not far from Bethel, and an invitation given to all who desired to be Methodists to resort thither. But being disappointed in this plan, Robert R. Roberts, the resident elder, came to Bethel, insisted on preaching to us and taking the spiritual charge of the congregation, for we were Methodists he was told he should come on some terms with the trustees; his answer was, that "He did not come to consult with Richard Allen or other trustees, but to inform the congregation, that on next Sunday afternoon, he would come and take the spiritual charge." We told him he could not preach for us under existing circumstances. However, at the appointed time he came, but having taken previous advice we had our preacher in the pulpit when he came, and the house was so fixed that he could not get but more than half way to the pulpit. Finding himself disappointed he appealed to those who came with him as witnesses, that "That man (meaning the preacher), had taken his appointment." Several respectable white citizens who knew the colored people had been ill-used, were present, and told us not to fear, for they would see us righted, and not suffer Roberts to preach in a forcible manner, after which Roberts went away.

The next elder stationed in Philadelphia was Robert Birch, who, following the example of his predecessor, came and published a meeting for himself. But the method just mentioned was adopted and he had to go away disappointed. In consequence of this, he applied to the Supreme Court for a writ of mandamus, to know why the pulpit was denied him. Being elder, this brought on a lawsuit, which ended in our favor. Thus by the Providence of God we were delivered

34

from a long, distressing and expensive suit, which could not be resumed, being determined by the Supreme Court. For this mercy we desire to be unfeignedly thankful.

About this time, our colored friends in Baltimore were treated in a similar manner by the white preachers and trustees, and many of them driven away who were disposed to seek a place of worship, rather than go to law.

Many of the colored people in other places were in a situation nearly like those of Philadelphia and Baltimore, which induced us, in April 1816, to call a general meeting, by way of Conference. Delegates from Baltimore and other places which met those of Philadelphia, and taking into consideration their grievances, and in order to secure the privileges, promote union and harmony among themselves, it was resolved: "That the people of Philadelphia, Baltimore, etc., etc., should become one body, under the name of the African Methodist Episcopal Church." We deemed it expedient to have a form of discipline, whereby we may guide our people in the fear of God, in the unity of the Spirit, and in the bonds of peace, and preserve us from that spiritual despotism which we have so recently experienced—remembering that we are not to lord it over God's heritage, as greedy dogs that can never have enough. But with long suffering and bowels of compassion, to bear each other's burdens, and so fulfill the Law of Christ, praying that our mutual striving together for the promulgation of the Gospel may be crowned with abundant success.

The God of Bethel heard her cries,
He let his power be seen;

He stopp'd the proud oppressor's frown,
And proved himself a King.

Thou sav'd them in the trying hour,
Ministers and councils joined,
And all stood ready to retain
That helpless church of Thine.

Bethel surrounded by her foes,
But not yet in despair,
Christ heard her supplicating cries;
The God of Bethel heard.

African Supplement

ARTICLES IMPROVING, amending and altering the articles of association of the "African Methodist Episcopal Church, commonly called and known by the name of Bethel Church," of the city of Philadelphia, by and with consent of two-thirds of the male members of said church:

ART. 1. It is hereby provided and declared: That so much of the fourth article of association, as requires the consent of the elder for the time being, to grant alienations or conveyances of the estate, real or personal, in this corporation, vested or to be vested, be altered and repealed, provided that no grant, alienation, conveyance, mortgage or pledge of the estate, real or personal, in the said corporation, vested or to be vested, shall be made by the said trustees or their successors, unless with consent of two-thirds of the regular male members of the church, of at least twenty-one years of age and one year's standing.

ART. 2. Whereas, some persons, members of Bethel church, having been duly suspended, upon complaint made of their having walked or having been expelled from the said church, have afterwards been received as members of the Methodist Episcopal Church elsewhere, and notwithstanding their suspension or expulsion as aforesaid, have claimed to be admitted into the private and close meetings of the said "Bethel church," by reason of notes of admission obtained in some other church, of which they have been received as members: it is hereby declared, that no such person or persons whatever, while so suspended or have been so expelled, nor any other person or persons, not being members of the said Methodist Episcopal Church, shall be admitted to commune, or to the love feasts, or any other close or private meeting whatever, held in said Bethel church or any other church or churches which may hereafter become the property of this corporation, unless with the consent of two-thirds of the trustees of said church for the time being.

ART. 3. It is hereby further provided and declared, that a majority of the trustees and official members, convened agreeably to notice, given at least one Sabbath day previously to such meeting, shall and may nominate and appoint one or more persons of the African race, to exhort and preach in Bethel church, and any other church or churches, which may hereafter become the property of this corporation, for such time and on such conditions as may be agreed on —provided that the exhorters and preachers so nominated and appointed shall have been regularly licensed by the Quarterly Meeting Conference of the Bethel church, or some one of the Methodist Episcopal churches elsewhere, and provided also, that the Elder of the Methodist Episcopal Church for the time being, may as heretofore claim, and shall have and possess, a right to preach once on every Sunday, and once during the course of the week, and no more, in any or all the houses set apart, by the aforesaid trustees or their successors of the said Bethel church.

ART. 4. It is hereby provided and declared, that the trustees of Bethel church, and their successors or a majority of them, may open the said church or any church or churches, that may hereafter become the property of this corporation, and may appoint and hold a religious meeting or meetings there, provided that no person or persons be admitted at such meeting or meetings to exhort or preach, unless they shall have been duly licensed thereto, conformably to the rules and discipline of the M. E. Church, or have leave of a majority of said trustees.

ART. 5. It is hereby further ordered and declared, that the elder of the Methodist Episcopal Church for the time being in Philadelphia, shall in no case receive any person as a member of Bethel church, nor shall any person be received as a member thereof, or being a member thereof, be suspended or expelled therefrom, unless by a majority of the trustees of said church, or their successors; and that in case said elder shall refuse or neglect to preach and exhort in the said church or churches, which shall hereafter become the property of this corporation, once every Sunday, and once during the course of the week, as is herein before provided, or shall neglect or refuse to attend therein, to administer the ordinances of Baptism and the Lord's Supper, in that case a majority of the trustees or their successors, may appoint any other person, duly qualified, according to the rules and discipline of the Methodist Episcopal Church, to officiate in the place instead of the elder so refusing or neglecting; and if the said elder shall neglect or refuse to attend any quarterly conference, love feast, or meeting for the trial of a disorderly member of said church, or any other meeting, public or private, duly appointed by a majority of the trustees or their successors, it shall be lawful for them nevertheless, with the concurrence of one or more of their colored brethren, duly licensed to exhort or preach by the quarterly meeting conference of Bethel church, or with the concurrence of any other person or persons, so licensed by the Methodist Episcopal Church, to hold such quarterly meeting conference or love feast, and to proceed in the trial of such disorderly members, and to suspend or expel him or her, as may be right and just, to license qualified persons to exhort and preach; and, finally, to transact all business, and to proceed in their affairs, temporal and spiritual, with the same effect, to all intents and purposes, as if the said elder was personally present and consented thereto.

ART. 6. It is hereby further agreed and declared, that the elder of the Methodist Episcopal Church, for the time being, of the city of Philadelphia, shall in no case nominate any person to preach in Bethel church, or in any church or churches, which shall hereafter become the property of said corporation; unless with the concurrence of a majority of the trustees of the said church, or their successors; and that any nomination made without the occurrence of said trustees, or a majority of them, shall be void.

ART. 7. And it is hereby agreed, provided and declared, that any article or provision in the "Articles of Association," of the trustees and members of the African Methodist Episcopal Church, called Bethel church, heretofore made and agreed on, inconsistent with, or altered by these present articles, shall be so far as they may be inconsistent or altered.

The subscribing trustees and members of the African Methodist Episcopal Church, called Bethel church, heretofore incorporated under the style and title of the African Methodist Episcopal Church of the city of Philadelphia, in the Commonwealth of Pennsylvania, which the said corporation as aforesaid formed and established, having herein specified the improvements, amendments and alterations which are desired, respectfully exhibit and present the same to Joseph B. McKean, Esq., Attorney General of the Commonwealth of Pennsylvania, and to the honorable judges of the Supreme Court of the said Commonwealth; in pursuance of an Act of Assembly, entitled, "An act to confer on certain associations of the citizens of this commonwealth the powers and immunities of corporations, or bodies politic in law." Passed the 6th day of April, 1791.

Acts of Faith

I BELIEVE, O God, that Thou art an eternal, incomprehensible spirit, infinite in all perfections; who didst make all things out of nothing, and dost govern them all by thy wise providence.

Let me always adore Thee with profound humility, as my Sovereign Lord; and help me to love and praise Thee with godlike affections and suitable devotion.

I believe that in the unity of the Godhead, there is a trinity of persons; that Thou art perfectly one and perfectly three; one essence and three persons. I believe, O blessed Jesus, that Thou art of one substance with the Father, the very and eternal God; that Thou didst take upon Thee our frail nature; that Thou didst truly suffer, and wert crucified, dead and buried, to reconcile us to thy Father and to be a sacrifice for sin.

I believe, that according to the types and prophecies, which went before, of Thee, and according to Thy own infallible prediction, Thou didst by Thy own power rise from the dead the third day, that Thou didst ascend into Heaven, that there Thou sittest on Thy throne of glory adored by angels and interceding for sinners.

I believe, that Thou hast instituted and ordained holy mysteries, as pledges of Thy love, and for a continual commemoration of Thy death; that Thou hast not only given Thyself to die for me, but to be my spiritual food and sustenance in that holy sacrament to my great and endless comfort. O may I frequently approach Thy altar with humility and devotion, and work in me all those holy and heavenly affections, which become the remembrance of a crucified Saviour.

I believe, O Lord, that Thou hast not abandoned me to the dim light of my own reason to conduct me to happiness, but that Thou hast revealed in the Holy Scriptures whatever is necessary for me to believe and practice, in order to my eternal salvation.

O, how noble and excellent are the precepts; how sublime and enlightening the truth; how persuasive and strong the motives; how powerful the assistance of Thy holy religion, in which Thou hast instructed me; my delight shall be in Thy statutes, and I will not forget Thy word.

I believe it is my greatest honor and happiness to be thy disciple; how miserable and blind are those that live without God in the world, who despise the light of Thy holy faith. Make me to part with all the enjoyments of life; nay, even life itself, rather than forfeit this jewel of great price. Blessed are the sufferings which are endured, happy is the death which is undergone for heavenly and immortal truth! I believe that Thou hast prepared for those that love Thee, everlasting mansions of glory; if I believe Thee, O, eternal happiness. Why does anything appear difficult that leads to Thee? Why should I not willingly resist unto blood to obtain Thee? Why do the vain and empty employments of life take such vast hold of us? O, perishing time! Why dost Thou thus bewitch and deceive me? O, blessed eternity! When shalt Thou be my portion for ever?

43

Acts of Hope

O, MY God! in all my dangers, temporal and spiritual, I will hope in thee who art Almighty power, and therefore able to relieve me; who art infinite goodness, and therefore ready and willing to assist me.

O, precious blood of my dear Redeemer! O, gaping wounds of my crucified Saviour! Who can contemplate the sufferings of God incarnate, and not raise his hope, and not put his trust in Him? What, though my body be crumbled into dust, and that dust blown over the face of the earth, yet I undoubtedly know my Redeemer lives, and shall raise me up at the last day; whether I am comforted or left desolate; whether I enjoy peace or am afflicted with temptations; whether I am healthful or sickly, succored or abandoned by the good things of this life, I will always hope in thee, O, my chiefest, infinite good.

Although the fig-tree shall not blossom, neither shall fruit be in the vines; although the labor of the olive shall fail, and the fields yield no meat; although the flock shall be cut off from the fold, and there shall be no herd in the stalls, yet I will rejoice in the Lord, I will joy in the God of my salvation.

What, though I mourn and am afflicted here, and sigh under the miseries of this world for a time, I am sure that my tears shall one day be turned into joy, and that joy none shall take from me. Whoever hopes for the great things in this world, takes pains to attain them; how can my hopes of everlasting life be well grounded, if I do not strive and labor for that eternal inheritance? I will never refuse the meanest labors, while I look to receive such glorious wages; I will never repine at any temporal loss, while I expect to gain such eternal rewards. Blessed hope! be thou my chief delight in life, and then I shall be steadfast and immovable, always abounding in the work of the Lord; be thou my comfort and support at the hour of death, and then I shall contentedly leave this world, as a captive that is released from his imprisonment.

Acts of Love

O, INFINITE amiableness! When shall I love thee without bounds? without coldness or interruption, which, alas! so often seize me here below? Let me never suffer any creature to be Thy rival, or to share my heart with Thee; let me have no other God, no other love, but only Thee.

Whoever loves, desires to please the beloved object; and according to the degree of love is the greatness of desire; make me, O God! diligent and earnest in pleasing Thee; let me cheerfully discharge the most painful and costly duties; and forsake friends, riches, ease and life itself, rather than disobey Thee.

Whoever loves, desires the welfare and happiness of the beloved object; but Thou, O dear Jesus, can'st receive no addition from my imperfect services; what shall I do to express my affection towards Thee? I will relieve the necessities of my poor brethren, who are members of Thy body; for he that loveth not his brother whom he has seen, how can he love God whom he hath not seen?

O, crucified Jesus! in whom I live, and without whom I die; mortify in me all sensual desires; inflame my heart with Thy holy love, that I may no longer esteem the vanities of this world, but place my affections entirely on Thee.

46

Let my last breath, when my soul shall leave my body, breathe forth love to Thee, my God; I entered into life without acknowledging Thee, let me therefore finish it in loving Thee; O let the last act of life be love, remembering that God is love.

A Narrative

of the Proceedings of the Colored People During the Awful Calamity in Philadelphia, in the Year 1793; and a Refutation of Some Censures Thrown upon Them in Some Publications.

By ABSALOM JONES AND RICHARD ALLEN

IN CONSEQUENCE of a partial representation of the conduct of the people, who were employed to nurse the sick in the calamitous state of the city of Philadelphia, we were solicited by a number of those who felt themselves injured thereby, and by the advice of several respectable citizens, to step forward and declare facts as they really were; and seeing that from our situation, on account of the charge we took upon us, we had it more fully and generally in our power to know and observe the conduct and behavior of those that were so employed.

Early in September, a solicitation appeared in the public papers to the people of color to come forward and assist the distressed, perishing and neglected sick; with a kind of assurance, that people of our color were not liable to take the infection; upon which we and a few others met and consulted how to act on so truly alarming and melancholy an occasion. After

48

some conversation, we found a freedom to go forth,
confiding in Him who can preserve in the midst of a
burning, fiery furnace. Sensible that it was our duty
to do all the good we could to our suffering fellow
mortals, we set out to see where we could be useful.
The first we visited was a man in Elmsley's Alley,
who was dying, and his wife lay dead at the time in
the house. There were none to assist but two poor,
helpless children. We administered what relief we
could, and applied to the overseers of the poor to have
the woman buried. We visited upwards of twenty
families that day—they were scenes of woe indeed!
The Lord was pleased to strengthen us and remove
all fear from us, and disposed our hearts to be as
useful as possible. In order the better to regulate
our conduct, we called on the mayor next day, to consult with him how to proceed so as to be most useful.
The first object he recommended was a strict attention to the sick and the procuring of nurses. This was
attended to by Absalom Jones and William Gray; and
in order that the distressed might know where to apply, the mayor advertised the public that upon application to them they would be supplied. Soon after,
the mortality increasing, the difficulty of getting a
corpse taken away was such, that few were willing
to do it when offered great rewards. The colored
people were looked to. We then offered our services in
the public papers, by advertising that we would remove the dead and procure nurses. Our services
were the production of real sensibility; we sought
not fee nor reward, until the increase of the disorder
rendered our labor so arduous, that we were not ade-
quate to the service we had assumed. The mortality
increasing rapidly, obliged us to call in the assistance
of five hired men in the awful charge of interring
the dead. They, with great reluctance, were prevail-

ing upon to join us. It was very uncommon, at this time, to find any one that would go near, much more handle a sick or dead person.

When the sickness became general, and several of the physicians died, and most of the survivors were exhausted by sickness or fatigue, that good man, Dr. Rush, called us more immediately to attend upon the sick, knowing that we could both bleed. He told us that we could increase our utility by attending to his instructions, and according directed us where to procure medicine duly prepared, with proper directions how to administer them, and at what stages of the disorder to bleed; and when we found ourselves incapable of judging what was proper to be done, to apply to him and he would, if able, attend them himself or send Edward Fisher, his pupil, which he often did; and Mr. Fisher manifested his humanity by an affectionate attention for their relief. This has been no small satisfaction to us; for we think that when a physician was not attainable, we have been the instruments in the hands of God, for saving the lives of some hundreds of our suffering fellow mortals.

We feel ourselves sensibly aggrieved by the censorious epithets of many who did not render the least assistance in the time of necessity, yet are liberal of their censure of us, for the prices paid for our services, when no one knew how to make a proposal to anyone they wanted to assist them. At first we made no charge but left it to those we served in removing their dead to give what they thought fit. We set no price until the reward was fixed by those we had served. After paying the people we had to assist us, our compensation was much less than many will believe.

We do assure the public that all the money we received for burying and for coffins, which we ourselves purchased and procured, has not defrayed the expense of wages which we had to pay those whom we employed to assist us. The following statement is accurately made:

Cash received—The whole amount of cash received for burying the dead, and for burying beds, is	£233	10	4
Cash paid for coffins, for which we received nothing	33	00	0
For the hire of five men, three of them 70 days each, and the other two 63 days each, at 22s. 6d. per day	378	00	0
	£411	00	0
Debts due us, for which we expect but little	£110	00	0
From this statement, for the truth of which we solemnly vouch, it is evident, and we sensibly feel the operation of the fact, that we are out of pocket	£177	9	8

Besides, the cost of hearses, the maintenance of our families for seventy days (being the period of our labors), and the support of the five hired men, during the respective times of their being employed; which expenses, together with sundry gifts we occasionally made to poor families, which might reasonably and properly be introduced, to show our actual situation with regard to profit; but it is enough to exhibit to the public, from the above specified items, of cash paid and cash received, without taking into view the other expenses, that by the employment we were engaged in we lost 177£. 9s. 8d. But if the other expenses, which we have actually paid, are added to that sum, how much then may we not say we have suffered? We leave the public to judge.

It may possibly appear strange to some who know how constantly we were employed, and that we should have received no more cash than 233£. 10s. 4d. But we repeat our assurance that this is the fact; and we add another, which will serve the better to explain it: we have buried several hundred of poor persons and strangers, for which service we have never received nor never asked any compensation.

We feel ourselves hurt most by a partial, censorious paragraph in Mr. Carey's second edition of his account of the sickness, etc., in Philadelphia, pages 76 and 77, where he asperses the blacks alone, for having taken the advantage of the distressed situation of the people.

That some extravagant prices were paid we admit; but how came they to be demanded? The reason is plain. It was with difficulty persons could be had to supply the wants of the sick as nurses; applications became more and more numerous; the consequence was, when we procured them at six dollars per week, and called upon them to go where they were wanted, we found they were gone elsewhere. Here was a disappointment. Upon inquiring the cause, we found they had been allured away by others, who offered greater wages, until they got from two to four dollars per day. We had no restraint upon the people. It was natural for people in low circumstances to accept a voluntary, bounteous reward; especially under the loathesomeness of many of the sick, when nature shuddered at the thought of the infection, and the task assigned was aggravated by lunacy and being left much alone with them. Had Mr. Carey been solicited to such an undertaking, for hire, query—what would he have demanded? But Mr. Carey, although chosen a member of that band of worthies who have so eminently distinguished themselves by their labors for the relief of the sick and helpless; yet, quickly after his election, left them to struggle with their arduous and hazardous task, by leaving the city. 'Tis true Mr. Carey was no hireling and had a right to flee, and, upon his return, to plead the cause of those who fled; yet, we think, he was wrong in giving so partial and injurious an account of the colored nurses; if they have taken advantage of the public distress, is it any more than he hath done of its desire for information? We believe he has made more money by the sale of his "Scraps" than a dozen of the greatest extortioners among the colored nurses. The great prices paid did not escape the observation of that worthy and vigilant magistrate, Matthew Clarkson, mayor of the city, and president of the committee. He sent us, and requested we would use our influence to lessen the wages of the nurses. But on informing him of the cause, i.e., that of the people over-bidding one another, it was concluded unnecessary to attempt anything on that head; therefore it was left to the people concerned. That there were some few colored people guilty of plundering the distressed we acknowledge; but in that they only are pointed out and made mention of, we esteem partial and injurious. We know as many whites who were guilty of it; but this is looked over, while the blacks are held up to censure. Is it a greater crime for a black to pilfer than for a white to privateer?

We wish not to offend; but when an unprovoked attempt is made to make us blacker than we are, it becomes less necessary to be over-cautious on that account; therefore we shall take the liberty to tell of the conduct of some of the whites.

We know that six pounds was demanded by and paid to a white woman, for putting a corpse into a coffin; and forty dollars was demanded and paid to four white men, for bringing it down the stairs.

Mr. and Mrs. Taylor both died in one night. A white woman had the care of them. After they were dead she called on Jacob Servoss, Esq., for her pay, demanding six pounds for laying them out. Upon seeing a bundle with her, he suspected she had pilfered. On searching her, Mr. Taylor's buckles were found in her pocket, with other things.

An elderly lady, Mrs. Malony, was given into the care of a white woman. She died. We were called to remove the corpse. When we came, the woman was lying so drunk that she did not know what we were doing; but we knew that she had one of Mrs. Malony's rings on her finger.

It is unpleasant to point out the bad and unfeeling conduct of any color; yet the defense we have undertaken obliges us to remark, that although hardly any of good character at that time could be procured, yet only two colored women were at that time in the hospital, and they were retained and the others discharged, when it was reduced to order and good government.

The bad consequences many of our color apprehend from a partial relation of our conduct are, that it will prejudice the minds of the people in general against us; because it is impossible that one individual can have knowledge of all; therefore at some future day, when some of the most virtuous that were upon most praiseworthy motives, induced to serve the sick, may fall into the service of a family that are strangers to him or her, and it is discovered that it is one of those stigmatized wretches, what may we suppose will be the consequence? Is it not reasonable to think the

54

person will be abhorred, despised and perhaps dismissed from employment, to their great disadvantage? would not this be hard? and have we not therefore sufficient reason to seek for redress? We can with certainty assure the public that we have seen more humanity, more real sensibility from the poor colored than from the poor whites. When many of the former, of their own accord, rendered services where extreme necessity called for it, the general part of the poor white people were so dismayed, that instead of attempting to be useful, they, in a manner, hid themselves. A remarkable instance of this: A poor, afflicted, dying man stood at his chamber window, praying and beseeching every one that passed by to help him to a drink of water. A number of white people passed, and instead of being moved by the poor man's distress, they hurried, as fast as they could, out of the sound of his cries, until at length a gentleman, who seemed to be a foreigner, came up. He could not pass by, but had not resolution enough to go into the house. He held eight dollars in his hand, and offered it to several as a reward for giving the poor man a drink of water, but was refused by every one, until a poor colored man came up. The gentleman offered the eight dollars to him, if he would relieve the poor man with a little water. "Master," replied the good-natured fellow, "I will supply the gentleman with water, but surely I will not take your money for it," nor could he be prevailed upon to accept his bounty. He went in, supplied the poor object with water, and rendered him every service he could.

A poor colored man, named Sampson, went constantly from house to house where distress was, and no assistance, without fee or reward. He was smitten with the disorder, and died. After his death, his family was neglected by those he had served.

Sarah Bass, a colored widow woman, gave all the assistance she could in several families, for which she did not receive anything; and when anything was offered her, she left it to the option of those she served.

A colored woman nursed Richard Mason and son. They died. Richard's widow, considering the risk the poor woman had run, and from observing the fears that sometimes rested on her mind, expected she would have demanded something considerable; but upon asking her what she demanded, her reply was, "fifty cents per day." Mrs. Mason intimated it was not sufficient for her attendance. She replied, that it was enough for what she had done, and would take no more. Mrs. Mason's feelings were such, that she settled an annuity of 6£ a year on her for life. Her name was Mary Scott.

An elderly, colored woman nursed———with great diligence and attention. When recovered, he asked what he must give her for her services—she replied, "a dinner, master, on a cold winter's day." And thus she went from place to place, rendering every service in her power, without an eye to reward.

A young colored woman was requested to attend one night upon a white man and his wife, who were very ill. No other person could be had. Great wages were offered her—she replied, "I will not go for money, if I go for money, God will see it and may make me take the disorder and die; but if I go and take no money, he may spare my life. She went about 9 o'clock, and found them both on the floor. She could procure no candle or other light, but stayed with them about two hours, and then left them. They both died that night. She was afterwards very ill with the fever. Her life was spared.

Caesar Cranchal, a man of color, offered his services to attend the sick, and said, "I will not take your money; I will not sell my life for money." It is said he died with the flux.

A colored lad, at the widow Gilpin's, was intrusted with his young master's keys, on his leaving the city, and transacted his business with the greatest honesty and despatch; having unloaded a vessel for him in the time, and loaded it again.

A woman that nursed David Bacon charged with exemplary moderation, and said she would not have any more.

It may be said in vindication of the conduct of those who discovered ignorance or incapacity in nursing, that it is, in itself, a considerable art derived from experience as well as the exercise of the finer feelings of humanity. This experience nine-tenths of those employed, it is probable, were wholly strangers to.

We do not recollect such acts of humanity from the poor, white people, in all the round we have been engaged in. We could mention many other instances of the like nature, but think it needless.

It is unpleasant for us to make these remarks, but justice to our color demands it. Mr. Carey pays William Gray and us a compliment; he says, our services and others of our color have been very great, etc. By naming us, he leaves those others in the hazardous state of being classed with those who are called the "vilest." The few that were discovered to merit public censure were brought to justice, which ought to have sufficed, without being canvassed over in his "Trifle" of a pamphlet; which causes us to be more particular, and endeavor to recall the esteem of the public for our friends and the people of color, as far as they may be found worthy; for we conceive, and experience proves it, that an ill name is easier given than taken away. We have many unprovoked enemies who begrudge us the liberty we enjoy, and are glad to hear of any complaint against our color, be it just or unjust; in consequence of which we are more earnestly endeavoring all in our power, to warn, rebuke and exhort our African friends to keep a conscience void of offense towards God and man; and at the same time, would not be backward to interfere, when stigmas or oppression appear pointed at or attempted against them unjustly; and we are confident we shall stand justified in the sight of the candid and judicious for such conduct.

We can assure the public that there were as many white as black people detected in pilfering, although the number of the latter, employed as nurses, was twenty times as great as the former, and that there is, in our opinion, as great a proportion of white as of black inclined to such practices; and it is rather to be admired that so few instances of pilfering and robbery happened, considering the great opportunities there were for such things. We do not know of more than five colored people suspected of anything clandestine, out of the great number employed. The people were glad to get any person to assist them. A colored person was preferred, because it was supposed they were not so likely to take the disorder. The most worthless were acceptable; so that it would have been no cause of wonder if twenty causes of complaint had occurred for one that hath. It has been alleged that many of the sick were neglected by the nurses; we do not wonder at it, considering their situation; in many instances up night and day, without any one to relieve them; worn down with fatigue and want of sleep they could not, in many cases, render that assistance which was needful. Where we visited, the causes of complaint on this score were not numerous. The case of the nurses, in many instances, were deserving of commiseration; the patient raging and frightful to behold. It has frequently required two persons to hold them from running away; others have made attempts to jump out of a window, in many chambers they were nailed down and the door kept locked to prevent them from running away or breaking their necks; others lay vomiting blood and screaming enough to chill them with horror. Thus were many of the nurses circumstanced, alone, until the patient died; then called away to another scene of distress, and thus have been, for a week or ten days, left to do the best they could, without any sufficient rest, many of them having some of their dearest connections sick at the time and suffering for want, while their husband, wife, father, mother, etc., have been engaged in the service of the white people. We mention this to show the difference between this and nursing in common cases. We have suffered equally with the whites; our distress hath been very great, but much unknown to the white people. Few have been the whites that paid attention to us, while the colored persons were engaged in others' service. We can assure the public that we have taken four and five colored people in a day to be buried. In several instances, when they have been seized with the sickness, while nursing, they have been turned out of the house, wandering and destitute, until they found shelter wherever they could (as many of them would not be admitted to their former homes), they have languished alone, and we know of one who even died in a stable. Others acted with more tenderness; when their nurses were taken sick, they had proper care taken of them at their houses. We know of two instances of this. It is even to this day a generally received opinion in this city, that our color was not so liable to the sickness as the whites. We hope our friends will pardon us for setting this matter in its true state.

The public was informed that in the West Indies and other places, where this terrible malady had been, it was observed that the blacks were not affected with it. Happy would it have been for you, and much more so for us, if this observation had been verified by our experience.

When the people of color had the sickness and died, we were imposed upon, and told it was not with the prevailing sickness, until it became too notorious to be denied; then we were told some few died, but not many. Thus were our services extorted at the peril of our lives. Yet you accuse us of extorting a little money from you.

The bill of mortality for the year 1793, published by Matthew Whitehead and John Ormrod, clerks, and Joseph Dolby, sexton, will convince any reasonable man that will examine it, that as many colored people died in proportion as others. In 1792 there were 67 of our color buried, and in 1793 it amounted to 305; thus the burials among us have increased more than fourfold. Was not this in a great degree the effects of the services of the unjustly vilified colored people?

Perhaps it may be acceptable to the reader to know how we found the sick affected by the sickness. Our opportunities of hearing and seeing them have been very great. They were taken with a chill, a head-ache, a sick stomach, with pains in their limbs and back. This was the way the sickness in general began; but all were not affected alike. Some appeared but slightly affected with some of those symptoms. What confirmed us in the opinion of a person being smitten was the color of their eyes. In some it raged more furiously than in others. Some have languished for seven and ten days, and appeared to get better the day, or some hours before they died, while others were cut off in one, two or three days; but their complaints were similar. Some lost their reason, and raged with all the fury, madness could produce, and died in strong convulsions; others retained their reason to the last, and seemed rather to fall asleep than die. We could not help remarking that the former were of strong passions, and the latter of a mild temper. Numbers died in a kind of dejection; they concluded they must go (so the phrase for dying was), and therefore in a kind of fixed, determined state of mind went off.

It struck our minds with awe to have application made by those in health, to take charge of them in their sickness, and of their funeral. Such applications have been made to us. Many appeared as though they thought they must die and not live; some have lain on the floor to be measured for their coffins and graves.

A gentleman called one evening to request a good nurse might be got for him when he was sick, and to superintend his funeral, and gave particular directions how he would have it conducted. It seemed a surprising circumstance; for the man appeared at the time to be in perfect health; but calling two or three days after, to see him, found a woman dead in the house, and the man so far gone, that to administer anything for his recovery was needless—he died that evening. We mention this as an instance of the dejection and despondence that took hold on the minds of thousands, and are of opinion that it aggravated the case of many; while others who bore up cheerfully got up again, that probably would otherwise have died.

When the mortality came to its greatest stage, it was impossible to procure sufficient assistance; therefore many, whose friends and relations had left them, died unseen and unassisted. We have found them in various situations—some lying on the floor, as bloody as if they had been dipped in it, without any appearance of their having had even a drink of water for their relief; others lying on a bed with their clothes on, as if they had come in fatigued and lain down to rest; some appeared as if they had fallen dead on the floor, from the position we found them in.

Surely our task was hard; yet through mercy we were enabled to go on.

One thing we observed in several instances: when we were called, on the first appearance of the disorder, to bleed, the person frequently, on the opening of a vein, and before the operation was near over, felt a change for the better, and expressed a relief in their chief complaints; and we made it a practice to take more blood from them than is usual in other cases. These, in a general way, recovered; those who omitted bleeding any considerable time, after being taken by the sickness, rarely expressed any change they felt in the operation.

We feel a great satisfaction in believing that we have been useful to the sick, and thus publicly thank Dr. Benjamin Rush for enabling us to be so. We have bled upwards of eight hundred people, and do declare we have not received to the value of a dollar and half therefor. We were willing to imitate the doctor's benevolence, who, sick or well, kept his house open day and night, to give what assistance he could in this time of trouble.

Several affecting instances occurred when we were engaged in burying the dead. We have been called to bury some, who, when we came, we found alone; at other places, we found a parent dead, and none but little innocent babes to be seen, whose ignorance led them to think their parent was asleep; on account of their situation and their little prattle, we have been so wounded and our feelings so hurt, that we almost concluded to withdraw from our undertaking; but, seeing others so backward, we still went on.

An affecting instance: A woman died; we were sent for to bury her. On our going into the house, and taking the coffin in, a dear little innocent accosted us with "Mamma is asleep—don't wake her!" but when she saw us put her into the coffin, the distress of the child was so great that it almost overcame us. When she demanded why we put her mamma in the box, we did not know how to answer her, but committed her to the care of a neighbor, and left her with heavy hearts. In other places, where we have been to take the corpse of a parent, and have found a group of little ones alone, some of them, in a measure, capable of knowing their situation; their cries, and the innocent confusion of the little ones, seemed almost too much for human nature to bear. We have picked up little children that were wandering they knew not where (whose parents had been cut off), and taken them to the orphan house; for at this time the dread that prevailed over people's minds was so general, that it was a rare instance to see one neighbor visit another, and friends, when they met in the streets, were afraid of each other; much less would they admit into their houses the distressed orphan that had been where the sickness was. This extreme seemed, in some instances, to have the appearance of barbarity. With reluctance we call to mind the many opportunities there were in the power of individuals to be useful to their fellow men, yet through the terror of the times were omitted.

A colored man riding through the street, saw a man push a woman out of the house; the woman staggered and fell on her face in the gutter; and was not able to turn herself. The colored man thought she was drunk, but observing that she was in danger of suffocation, alighted, and taking the woman up, found her perfectly sober, but so far gone with the disorder that she was not able to help herself. The hard-hearted man that threw her down, shut the door and left her. In such a situation she might have perished in a few minutes. We heard of it, and took her to Bush Hill. Many of the white people, who ought to be patterns for us to follow after, have acted in a manner that would make humanity shudder. We remember an instance of cruelty, which, we trust, no colored man would be guilty of: Two sisters, orderly, decent, white women, were sick with the fever. One of them recovered, so as to come to the door. A neighboring white man saw her, and in an angry tone asked her if her sister was dead or not? She answered, "No," upon which he replied, "Damn her, if she don't die before morning, I will make her die!" The poor woman, shocked at such an expression from this monster of a man, made a modest reply, upon which he snatched up a tub of water, and would have dashed it over her, if he had not been prevented by a colored man. He then went and took a couple of fowls out of a coop (which had been given them for nourishment), and threw them into an open alley. He had his wish; the poor woman that he would make die, died that night.

A white man threatened to shoot us, if we passed by his house with a corpse. We buried him three days after.

We have been pained to see the widows come to us, crying and wringing their hands, and in very great distress, on account of their husbands' death; having nobody to help them, they were obliged to come and get their husbands buried. Their neighbors were afraid to go to their help, or to condole with them. We ascribe such unfriendly conduct to the frailty of human nature.

Notwithstanding the compliment Mr. Carey hath paid us, we have found reports spread of our taking between one and two hundred beds from houses where people died. Such slanderers as these, who propagate such willful lies, are dangerous, although unworthy; and we wish, if any person hath the least suspicion of us, they would endeavor to bring us to the punishment which such atrocious conduct must deserve; and by this means the innocent will be cleared from reproach, and the guilty known.

We shall now conclude with the following proverb, which we think applicable to those of our color, who exposed their lives in the late afflicting dispensation:

> God and a soldier all men do adore
> In time of war and not before;
> When the war is over, and all things righted,
> God is forgotten, and the soldier slighted.

To Matthew Clarkson, Esq., Mayor of the City of Philadelphia

SIR—FOR the personal respect we bear you, and for the satisfaction of the mayor, we declare, that to the best of our remembrance we had the care of the following beds, and no more:

Two, belonging to James Starr, we buried; upon taking them up, we found one damaged, the blankets, &c., belonging to it were stolen. It was refused to be accepted of by his son Moses. It was buried again, and remains so, for aught we know; the other was returned and accepted of.

We buried two belonging to Samuel Fisher, merchant; one of them was taken up by us to carry a sick person on to Bush Hill, and there left; the other was buried in a grave, under a corpse.

Two beds were buried for Thomas Willing—one, six feet deep, in his garden, and lime and water thrown upon it; the other was in the Potter's field, and further knowledge of it we have not.

We burned one bed, with other furniture and clothing, belonging to the late mayor, Samuel Powell, on his farm on the west side of Schuylkill river. We buried one of his beds.

For—Dickinson we buried a bed in a lot of Richard Allen, which we have good cause to believe was stolen.

One bed was buried for a person in Front Street, whose name is unknown to us—it was buried in the Potter's field by a person employed for the purpose. We told him he might take it up again, after it had been buried a week, and apply it to his own use, as he said that he had lately been discharged from the hospital and had none to lie on.

Thomas Leiper's two beds were buried in the Potter's field and remained there a week, and then taken up by us for the use of the sick that we took to Bush Hill, and left there.

We buried one for _____ Smith, in the Potter's field, which was returned, except the furniture, which we believe was stolen.

One other we buried, for _____ Davis, in Vine Street; it was buried near Schuylkill, and we believe continues so.

A bed from _____ Guest, in Second street, was buried in the Potter's field, and is there yet for anything we know.

One bed we buried in the Presbyterian burial ground, the corner of Pine and Fourth streets, and we believe was taken up by the owner, Thomas Mitchell.

_____ Milligan, in Second street, had a bed buried by us in the Potter's field. We have no further knowledge of it.

This is a true statement of matters respecting the beds, as far as we were concerned. We never undertook the charge of more than their burial, knowing they were liable to be taken away by evil-minded persons. We think it beneath the dignity of an honest man (although injured in his reputation by wicked and envious persons), to vindicate or support his character by an oath or legal affirmation. We fear not our enemies; let them come forward with their

THE LIFE EXPERIENCE AND GOSPEL LABORS

charges; we will not flinch; and if they can fix any crime upon us, we refuse not to suffer.

Sir, you have cause to believe our lives were endangered in more cases than one, in the time of the late mortality, and that we were so discouraged, that had it not been for your persuasion, we would have relinquished our disagreeable and dangerous employments; and we hope there is no impropriety in soliciting a certificate of your approbation of our conduct, so far as it hath come to your knowledge.

With an affectionate regard and esteem.

We are your friends,

ABSALOM JONES
RICHARD ALLEN.

January 7th, 1794.

Having, during the prevalence of the late malignant disorder, had almost daily opportunities of seeing the conduct of Absalom Jones and Richard Allen, and the people employed by them to bury the dead: I with cheerfulness give this testimony of my approbation of their proceedings, so far as they came under my notice. Their diligence, attention and decency of deportment, afforded me, at the time, much satisfaction.

MATTHEW CLARKSON, Mayor.

Philadelphia, Jan. 23rd, 1794.

An Address
To Those Who Keep Slaves and Approve the Practice

THE JUDICIOUS part of mankind, will think it unreasonable, that a superior good conduct is looked for from our race, by those who stigmatize us as men, whose baseness is incurable and may therefore be held in a state of servitude, that a merciful man would not doom a beast to; yet you try what you can to prevent our rising from a state of barbarism you represent us to be in; but we can tell you from a degree of experience, that a black man, although reduced to the most abject state human nature is capable of, short of real madness, can think, reflect and feel injuries, although it may not be with the same degree of keen resentment and revenge that you, who have been and are our great oppressors would manifest, if reduced to the pitiable condition of a slave. We believe if you would try the experiment of taking a few black children, and cultivate their minds with the same care and let them have the same prospect in view as to living in the world, as you would wish for your own children, you would find upon the trial, they were not inferior in mental endowments. I do not wish to make you angry, but excite your attention to consider how hateful slavery is in the sight of that God who hath destroyed kings and princes for their oppression of the poor slaves. Pharaoh and his princes, with the posterity of King Saul, were destroyed by the protector and avenger of slaves. Would you not suppose the Israelites to be utterly unfit for freedom and that it was impossible for them to obtain to any degree of excellence? Their history shows how slavery had debased their spirits. Men must be wilfully blind and extremely partial, that cannot see the contrary effects of liberty and slavery upon the mind of man: I truly confess the vile habits often acquired in a state of servitude, are not easily thrown off; the example of the Israelites shows, who with all that Moses could do to reclaim them from it, still continued in their habits more or less; and why will you look for better from us? why will you look for grapes from thorns, or figs from thistles? It is in our posterity enjoying the same privileges with your own, that you ought to look for better things.

When you are pleaded with, do not you reply as Pharaoh did, "Wherefore do ye, Moses and Aaron, let the people from their work, behold the people of the land now are many, and you make them rest from their burthens." We wish you to consider, that God himself was the first pleader of the cause of slaves.

That God, who knows the hearts of all men, and the propensity of a slave to hate his oppressor, hath strictly forbidden it to his chosen people, "Thou shalt not abhor an Egyptian, because thou wast a stranger in his land." Deut. 23, 7. The meek and humble Jesus, the great pattern of humanity and every other virtue that can adorn and dignify men, hath commanded to love our enemies; to do good to them that hate and despitefully use us. I feel the obligations; I wish to impress them on the minds of our colored brethren, and that we may all forgive you, as we wish to be forgiven; we think it a great mercy to have all anger and bitterness removed from our minds. I appeal to your own feelings, if it is not very disquieting to feel yourselves under the dominion of wrathful disposition.

If you love your children, if you love your country, if you love the God of love, clear your hands from slaves; burthen not your children or your country with them. My heart has been sorry for the blood shed of the oppressors, as well as the oppressed; both appear guilty of each other's blood, in the sight of him who hath said, "He that sheddeth man's blood, by man shall his blood be shed."

Will you, because you have reduced us to the unhappy condition our color is in, plead our incapacity for freedom, and our contented condition under oppression, as a sufficient cause for keeping us under the grievous yoke? I have shown the cause, I will also show why they appear contented as they can in your sight, but the dreadful insurrections they have made when opportunity has offered, is enough to convince a reasonable man that great uneasiness and not contentment is the inhabitant of their hearts. God himself hath pleaded their cause; He hath from time to time raised up instruments for that purpose, sometimes mean and contemptible in your sight, at other times He hath used such as it hath pleased him, with whom you have not thought it beneath your dignity to contend. Many have been convinced of their error, condemned their former conduct, and become zealous advocates for the cause of those whom you will not suffer to plead for themselves.

To the People of Color

FEELING AN engagement of mind for your welfare, I address you with an affectionate sympathy,
having been a slave, and as desirous of freedom as
any of you; yet the bands of bondage were so strong
that no way appeared for my release; yet at times a
hope arose in my heart that a way would open for
it; and when my mind was mercifully visited with the
feeling of the love of God, then these hopes increased,
and a confidence arose that he would make for my en-
largement; and as a patient waiting was necessary,
I was sometimes favored with it, at other times I was
very impatient. Then the prospect of liberty almost
vanished away, and I was in darkness and perplexity.

I mention experience to you, that your hearts may
not sink at the discouraging prospects you may have,
and that you may put your trust in God, who sees your
condition, and as a merciful father pitieth his children,
so doth God pity them that love Him; and as your
hearts are inclined to serve God, you will feel an
affectionate regard towards your masters and mis-
tresses, so called, and the whole family in which you
live. This will be seen by them, and tend to promote
your liberty, especially with such as have feeling
masters; and if they are otherwise, you will have the
favor and love of God dwelling in your hearts, which
you will value more than anything else, which will
be a consolation in the worst condition you can be in,

and no master can deprive you of it; and as life is short and uncertain, and the chief end of our having a being in this world is to be prepared for a better, I wish you to think of this more than anything else; then you will have a view of that freedom which the sons of God enjoy; and if the troubles of your condition end with your lives, you will be admitted to the freedom which God hath prepared for those of all colors that love him. Here the power of the most cruel master ends, and all sorrow and tears are wiped away.

To you who are favored with freedom, let your conduct manifest your gratitude toward the compassionate masters who have set you free; and let no rancour or ill-will lodge in your breast for any bad treatment you may have received from any. If you do, you transgress against God, who will not hold you guiltless. He would not suffer it even in his beloved people Israel; and you think he will allow it unto us? Many of the white people have been instruments in the hands of God for our good even such as have held us in captivity, are now pleading our cause with earnestness and zeal; and I am sorry to say, that too many think more of the evil than of the good they have received, and instead of taking the advice of their friends, turn from it with indifference. Much depends upon us for the help of our color—more than many are aware. If we are lazy and idle, the enemies of freedom plead it as a cause why we ought not to be free, and say we are better in a state of servitude, and that giving us our liberty would be an injury to us; and by such conduct we strengthen the bands of oppression and keep many in bondage who are more worthy than ourselves. I entreat you to consider the obligations we lie under to help forward the cause of freedom. He who knows how bitter the cup is of which

73

the slave hath to drink, O, how ought we to feel for those who yet remain in bondage! Will even our friends excuse—will God pardon us—for the part we act in making strong the hands of the enemies of our color?

A Short Address to the Friends
of Him Who Hath no Helper:

I FEEL an inexpressible gratitude towards you who
have engaged in the cause of the African race; you
have wrought a deliverance for many from more than
Egyptian bondage; your labors are unremitted for
their complete redemption from the cruel subjection
they are in. You feel our afflictions; you sympathize
with us in the heartrending distress, when the husband is separated from the wife, and the parents from
the children, who are never more to meet in this
world. The tear of sensibility trickles from your eye
to see the sufferings that keep us from increasing.
Your righteous indignation is roused at the means
taken to supply the place of the murdered babe; you
see our race more effectually destroyed than was in
Pharaoh's power to effect upon Israel's sons; you
blow the trumpet against the mighty evil; you make
the tyrants tremble; you strive to raise the slave to
the dignity of a man; you take our children by the
hand to lead them in the path of virtue, by your
care of our education; you are not ashamed to call
the most abject of our race brethren, children of one
Father, who hath made of one blood all the nations
of the earth. You ask for this nothing for yourselves;
nothing but what is worthy the cause you are engaged in; nothing but that we would be friends to
ourselves, and not strengthen the bands of oppression

by an evil conduct, when led out of the house of bondage. May He, who hath arisen to plead our cause and engaged you as volunteers in the service, add to your numbers, until the princes shall come forth from Egypt, and Ethiopia stretch out her hands unto God.

RICHARD ALLEN.

Ye ministers that are called to preaching,
  Teachers and exhorters too,
Awake! behold your harvest wasting;
  Arise! there is no rest for you.

To think upon that strict commandment
  That God has on his teachers laid
The sinners' blood, who die unwarned,
  Shall fall upon their shepherd's head.

But, O! dear brethren, let's be doing—
  Behold the nations in distress;
The Lord of hosts forbid their ruin,
  Before the day of grace is past.

We read of wars and great commotions,
  Before the great and dreadful day;
Oh! sinners, turn your sinful courses,
  And trifle not your time away.

But oh! dear sinners, that's not all that's dreadful;
  You must before your God appear,
To give an account of your transactions,
  And how you spent your time when here.

Our Saviour's first and great work was that of the salvation of men's souls; yet we find that of the multitudes who came or were brought to Him laboring under sickness and disorders, He never omitted one opportunity of doing good to their bodies, or sent
76

away one that applied to Him without a perfect cure; though sometimes, for the trial of their faith, He suffered Himself to be importuned. And that He also often administered to the necessities of the poor in money is plain from several passages of His life, one of which may suffice for the present, viz.: When Satan had entered into Judas, and our blessed Saviour had said, "That thou doest do quickly"; none of the other disciples knew for what intent He had so spoken; for some of them thought, because Judas had the bag or common purse, that either He had ordered him to buy what was necessary against the feast, or (as was usual, no doubt, otherwise they could not have supposed it) that he would give something to the poor.

To this unanswerable proof from our Saviour's practice may be added His repeated precepts and exhortations; for His examples and doctrines were always of a piece. "A new commandment," says he, "I give unto you, that ye love one another. By this shall all men know that ye are my disciples, if ye have love one to another. This is my commandment, that ye love one another as I have loved you. Greater love hath no man than this, that a man lay down his life for his friends. I say unto you which hear, love your enemies, and do good to them which hate you; bless them that curse you and pray for them which despitefully use you. Love your enemies, and do good and lend, hoping for nothing again, and your reward shall be great and ye shall be the children of the Highest; for he is kind to the unthankful and to the evil. Be ye therefore merciful as your Father also is merciful." From these few passages may be collected the nature, extent and necessity of Christian charity. In its nature it is pure and disinterested, remote from all hopes or views of worldly return or recompense from the persons we relieve. We are to do good and lend, hoping for nothing again. In its extent it is unlimited and universal; and, though it requires that an especial regard be had to our fellow Christians, is confined to no persons, countries or places, but takes in all mankind, strangers as well as relations or acquaintances, enemies as well as friends, the evil and unthankful, as well as the good and grateful. It has no other measure than the love of God to us, who gave His only begotten Son, and the love of our Saviour, who laid down His life for us, even whilst we were his enemies. It reaches not only to the good of the soul, but also to such assistance as may be necessary for the supply of the bodily wants of our fellow creatures.

And the absolute necessity of practising this duty is the very same with that of being Christians; this being the only sure mark by which we may be known and distinguished from such as are not Christians or disciples of Christ. "By this shall all men know that ye are my disciples, if ye have love one to another."

Hearken to St. Paul, speaking of this most excellent way or duty, and then judge ye, my brethren, of the necessity of putting it in practice:

"Though I speak with the tongue of men and angels and have not charity, I am become as a sounding brass or a tinkling cymbal. And though I have the gift of prophecy, and understand all mysteries, and all knowledge, and though I have all faith, so that I could remove mountains, and have not charity, I am nothing. And though I bestow all my goods to feed the poor, and though I give my body to be burned, and have not charity, it profiteth nothing."

But these articles will receive a considerable light from the consideration of the second point, viz., the benefits and advantages arising from the practice of Christian charity.

In which as the present occasion more especially points out to us, we may take a short, general view of the advantages and benefits attending the exercise of that particular branch of Christian charity, which consists in the applying and bestowing some part of our substance or the produce of our labors towards the relief and support of the poor and needy; or in contributing towards such works of piety and mercy as are intended and contrived for the real good and bettering the condition of our indigent brethren, either by public or private ways of charity. And by this we improve our talents to the glory of God and the welfare of our own immortal souls.

Consider, my brethren, that all we have and are is entrusted to us by Almighty God. In him we live, move and have our being. The earth is the Lord's, and the fulness (or plenty) thereof. We are consequently no more than his servants or stewards; the talents are all his; it is his substance that is distributed by him among us, to some more, to some less, as it has pleased him to entrust us with our own several portions of dividends; and to him we must give an account at the great day of reckoning, for every penny—for the improvement as well as for the principal.

Our blessed Lord has not committed his goods to us as a dead stock, to be hoarded up, or to lie unprofitably in our own hands. He expects that we shall put them out to proper and beneficial uses, and raise them to an advanced value by doing good with them, as often as we have opportunity of laying them out upon the real interest and welfare of his poor children and subjects. By doing acts of mercy and charity, we acknowledge our dependence upon God, and his absolute right to whatever we possess through his bounty and goodness; we glorify him in his creatures, and reverence him by a due and cheerful obedience to his commands. By applying our substance to the pomps and vanities of this wicked world, or the gratification of the sinful lusts of the flesh, we deny God's right to what he hath thought fit to place in our hands; and disown him as our master by laying out his substance in ways expressly contrary to his orders; we thereby gratify Satan, whom we renounced at our baptism, and most shamefully dishonor our Maker by the abuse of his talents. When, therefore, we are called to a reckoning at that awful tribunal before which the most wealthy and powerful upon earth shall appear as naked and friendless as the poorest beggar, and when nothing but the goodness of our cause, and the mercy of our judge, can afford us the least support if in that strict and solemn examination we have no better accounts to give in, than—so much laid out in luxury and extravagance, rapine and oppression; so much in a vexatious, litigious lawsuit, or other idle, useless diversions, but little or nothing in charity. Shillings and pounds upon our vanity and folly, but scarce a few pence upon doing good! With what shame and confusion shall we hang down our heads, and wish for rocks and mountains to cover us, not only from the view of our justly offended master, but from the eyes of angels and men, all witnesses of our disgrace!

Some may, perhaps, say, "Well, I have refrained from debauchery, folly and idleness; I have earned my honest penny, and kept it, and laid up a comfortable provision for my family." Be it so; this is laudable and praiseworthy, and it were to be wished that many more in this country would do so much. But may not such a one be asked, have you been charitable withal? have you been as industrious in laying up treasures in heaven, as you have been in hoarding up the perishable riches of this world? Have you stretched out your hand, as you had opportunity, beyond the circle of your own house and family? Have your poorer neighbors cause to bless you for your kind and charitable assistance? Have you dedicated any portion of your labors to God, who blessed them, by doing good to any besides your own? Has the stranger, the widow or the fatherless ever tasted of your bounty? If you have never done things of this kind, but have hitherto slighted, overlooked or put off occasions of this sort, your talent is as yet hid in a napkin, it lies yet buried in the ground, huddled up within yourself. And consider further, that the real poor and needy are Christ's representatives. We cannot, surely, doubt of this, if we look into our Saviour's own account of the last judgment, 25th chap. of St. Matthew's Gospel, which plainly shows us that the inquiry at that great and solemn day will be very particular about our works of mercy and charity: "Inasmuch as ye have done, or inasmuch as ye have not done it to the least of these, my brethren, ye have done, or ye have not done it to me." When, therefore, an object of charity or an opportunity of doing good, presents itself, the prudent Christian will not once deliberate, shall I relieve this man or this woman? shall I assist this widow, this orphan, or this poor child? No, he rather considers it as a demand made upon him by Christ himself, and would be as much afraid to delay or refuse payment in such case, as if he saw his Lord and Saviour coming to ask it of him in person. The question, therefore, with him is this: Do not the holy Scriptures expressly teach me that whatsoever I do to my brethren who stand in need, will be reckoned to me as if I had done it to Christ himself? Can I relieve them without relieving Him, or can I neglect them without slighting Him? What hope could I have of being received and accepted of Him at the last day, or that He will then hearken to my cries for mercy and forgiveness, should I be regardless of the requests He now makes to me by His members and representatives? I earnestly desire my Lord may have mercy upon me; therefore will I cheerfully show mercy to this His brother, however little or contemptible he may appear. I ardently wish my Lord may show goodness to me at the great day of reckoning; therefore will I seize the present opportunity of doing good, which He, in His good will towards me, now offers to my acceptance.

The accustoming ourselves to those acts, separates our affections from earthly things; learns us to sit loose to the world and secures us treasures in heaven.

To people who are heartily in love with this world; who can see no greater happiness than wealth or power upon earth can afford them, such advantages, I own, are in no sort alluring. To talk of placing their affections upon possessions beyond the grave, or of lessening their present gains, in hopes of future benefits, is much to the same purpose as setting a most beautiful prospect before a blind man, or the most delicate meats before one who has lost his palate.

The person who has a due regard to his eternal salvation; who knows by experience how apt the love of earthly things is to draw off his affections from those of a heavenly nature; who remembers that he ought not to love the world, nor the things that are in the world, because the friendship of this world is enmity with God, and that whosoever will be a friend (or lover) of the world is the enemy of God; who reflects that a time will come when he must part with all that is dear to him here; how necessary it is, therefore, to wean his mind from these perishable things, that they may give him no pain or uneasiness in quitting them, and is convinced that the whole world is of infinitely less value than the least inheritance in the kingdom of heaven. Such a one is always prepared to exercise himself in acts of mercy and charity; giving up a part, whenever opportunity offers of doing good, in token of his readiness to give up the whole whensoever God shall please to call upon him for it; and rejoices in the means afforded him of laying up treasures subject to no waste, rapine or corruption, at the small expense of a trifling sum here; nay, is ready, should it appear necessary, to follow the advice of our Saviour to his little flock, "Sell that ye have, and give alms; provide yourselves bags which wax not old, a treasure in the heavens which faileth not."

In short, the love of this world is a heavy weight upon the soul, which chains her down and prevents her flight towards heaven. Habitual acts of charity loosen her from it by degrees, and help her in her struggle to disengage herself and mount upwards.

A dying person would give the whole world, were it in his possession, for any rational assurance of acceptance with God, and an inheritance in the kingdom of heaven; why then will any man who knows he must one day die, neglect the insuring it to himself by such works of mercy in his health and strength, as he may be assured will help him to mercy in a dying hour? "Blessed are the merciful," saith our dear Redeemer, "for they shall obtain mercy."

Another advantage arising from acts of mercy and charity is, that they secure us the blessing and protection of heaven.

"Blessed is he," saith King David, "who considereth the poor and needy; the Lord will deliver him in the time of trouble. The Lord will preserve him and keep him alive, and he shall be blessed upon the earth, and Thou wilt not deliver him into the will of his enemies. The Lord will strengthen him upon the bed of languishing; Thou wilt make all his bed in his sickness." To be slow and uneasy at almsgiving, argues a strong distrust in Providence, either that God cannot or will not make up to us what we thus bestow. To suppose he cannot, is to deny his Almighty power and consequently that he is God. To imagine he will not, is to suspect his truth, who has not only promised eternal treasures in heaven, but has also engaged his sure word that he will repay it, even upon earth, as if it were lent to himself. He that hath pity upon the poor lendeth to the Lord, and that which he hath borrowed, he will repay him again.

With how great reason did our Saviour so solemnly charge his disciples to beware of covetousness, since we see it borders so nearly upon infidelity. How strangely inconsistent is the narrow-hearted man with himself, with his own settled principles! He desires a blessing upon all that he has; he earnestly wishes for wealth and prosperity, yet cannot find in his heart to lay out a little of what he has to secure that blessing, that prosperity he aims at for himself and family, in doing these good and charitable actions which Providence throws in his way, and which God has assured him will purchase it! How much more rationally does the openhearted, benevolent Christian act, and upon what sure and steady principles does he proceed! This trifle, says he to himself, which I now bestow, may possibly be of some small, present inconvenience to me, but it is given to God, and He will never suffer me to feel the want of it. My Saviour has kindly insured to me whatever is necessary in this world, by promising, that if I seek the kingdom of God and his righteousness, and these things, which others are toiling and sweating after, often to no purpose but vexation and disappointment, shall be added unto me. Here are both earthly and heavenly blessings laid before me, so that I cannot fail of a return from God, though he hath expressly ordered me to hope for nothing again from those I give to. I shall therefore assuredly reap according to my sowing—in this world, if God sees it good for me, but most certainly in the blessings of the next, if I grow not faint or impatient. My alms will ascend up before God for a memorial; and as he has taken the payment upon himself, I am convinced that even a cup of cold water thus bestowed, by those who have no more to give, will not lose its reward; for Jesus has promised, and in him all the promises of God are yea and amen.

Having thus gone through the proposed heads, and shown the nature, the extent and necessity of Christian charity; having pointed out the benefits and advantages arising from the practice of it, and how it secures to us the blessings, both of this world and the world to come, it now remains that some common objections be considered, with a short application to the present design. Objections, I know, are many, and each person unwilling to contribute towards a charitable proposal will find out one of some kind or other, to ward off the blow that seems to aim at his very heart. Numerous, however, as they are, they appear so trifling as to deserve little particular consideration and might well enough be examined in bulk.

All objections to charitable contributions may well be supposed to arise from covetousness, or an unwillingness to part with the present penny. Covetousness is indeed a Goliath, a giant of the first magnitude, which is always ready to defy and set at naught the best formed arguments and motives drawn from reason and Scripture, all the armies of the living God. All the common pretences to prudence in the manner or time of giving charity, all hints of reserving it for better purposes, generally center in covetousness, in the love of money; and how wretched a fruit is to be expected from the root of all evil, as St. Paul expressly calls it, let every one judge for himself.

But the answer to all such pretences of prudence in bestowing, in short, is this: you may be deceived in the object, but you never can be deceived in your intention of charity, be the object ever so undeserving; nay, should I bestow money upon one in apparent necessity, who might abuse it to ill purposes, yet the good intention sanctifies my gift, consecrates it to God, and insures me a blessing, because it was done in His name and for His sake; while the whole abuse of it rests upon the guilty head of the vile person who thus basely misapplies my good deed. It may, indeed, be a reasonable objection against my giving a second time to that same person, but can be no excuse to me for withholding my hand from the relief of any other object which may appear another time to be in real want of charity.

And O! consider what a joyful thing it must be for a person in a dying hour to have a conscience free from offense, and to see their blessed Saviour, with His arms stretched out, ready to receive them when their breath leaves the body, and saying, "Well done, thou good and faithful servant; thou hast been faithful over a few things, I will make thee ruler over many things; enter thou into the joy of the Lord." Are not these, my brethren and sisters, pleasures worth seeking after? Are not these privileges, this freedom and these possessions of far more value than thousands of worlds like this we live in, which we must all leave in a short time, and cannot carry with us into another life? And can you ever sufficiently admire the goodness of God, or ever be thankful enough to Him for His loving kindness, who hath set these glories and these enjoyments as much within

the reach of the poorest slave as of the greatest prince
alive? For it is not power and high station that can
purchase these heavenly possessions; they are only
to be gained by goodness and serving of God; and
the lowest of us can serve God as well as the richest
person here below, and, by that means, may adorn the
doctrine of the Lord your God in all things, and
bring more honor to Christ than many of higher rank
and condition, who are not so careful of their souls
as you may be.

When, therefore, we shall leave this impertinent and
unsociable world, and all our good old friends that
are gone to Heaven before us, shall meet us as soon
as we are landed upon the shore of eternity, and with
infinite congratulations for our safe arrival, shall conduct us into the company of patriarchs, prophets,
apostles and martyrs and introduce us into an intimate
acquaintance with them, and with all those brave and
generous souls, who, by their glorious examples, have
recommended themselves to the world; when we shall
be familiar friends with angels and archangels; and
all the courtiers of heaven shall call us brethren and
bid us welcome to their Master's joy, and we shall
be received into their glorious society with all the
tender endearments and caresses of those heavenly
lovers; what a mighty addition to our happiness will
this be! There are, indeed, some other additions to the
happiness of Heaven, such as the glory and magnifi-
cence of the place, which is the highest Heaven, or
the upper and purer tracts of the ether, which our
Saviour calls Paradise.

In the temper of every wicked mind there is a
strong antipathy to the pleasures of Heaven, which,
being all chaste, pure and spiritual, can never agree
with the vitiated palate of a base and degenerate soul.
For what concord can there be between a spiteful and

devilish spirit and the fountain of all love and goodness? Between a sensual and carnalized one, that understands no other pleasures but only those of the flesh, and those pure and virgin spirits, that neither eat nor drink, but live for ever upon wisdom, holiness, love and contemplation? Certainly till our mind is contempered to the heavenly state, and we are of the same disposition with God and angels and saints, there is no pleasure in Heaven that can be agreeable to us. For as in the main we shall be of the same temper and disposition when we come into the other life as we are when we leave this, it being unimaginable how a total change should be wrought in us merely by passing out of one world into another, and, therefore, as in this world, it is likeness that does congregate and associate beings together, so, doubtless, it is in the other world too; so that if we carry with us thither our wicked and devilish dispositions (as we shall certainly do, unless we subdue and mortify them here), there will be no company fit for us to associate with, but only the devilish and damned ghosts of wicked men, with whom our wretched spirits, being already joined by a likeness of nature, will mingle themselves as soon as ever they are excommunicated from the society of mortals.

For whither should they flock but to the birds of their own feather? with whom should they associate but with those malignant spirits, to whom they are already joined by a community of nature? So that, supposing that when they land in eternity, it were left to their own choice to go to heaven or hell, into the society of the blessed or the damned, it is plain that heaven would be no place for them; that the air of that bright region of eternal day would never agree with their black and hellish natures; for, alas! what should they do among those blessed beings that inhabit it? To those godlike natures, divine contemplation and heavenly employments, they have so great a repugnancy and aversion? So that, besides the having a right to Heaven, it is necessary to our enjoying it, that we should be antecedently disposed and qualified for it. And it being thus, God hath been graciously pleased to make those very virtues the condition of our right to Heaven, which are the proper dispositions and qualifications of our spirits for it, that so, with one and the same labor, we might entitle ourselves and qualify ourselves to enjoy it.

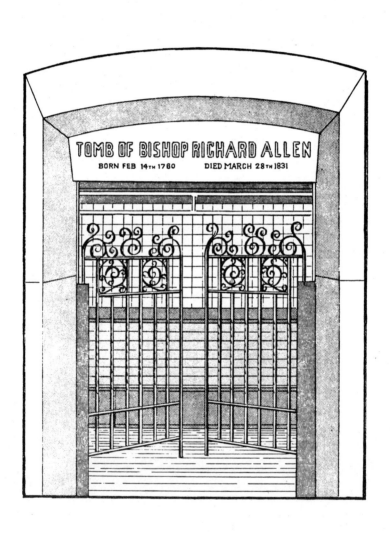

TOMB OF BISHOP RICHARD ALLEN

BORN FEB 14TH 1760   DIED MARCH 28TH 1831

Index of Proper Names